PURSUED by a
Relentless GOD

PURSUED by a
Relentless GOD

SHAWN BRACE

Pacific Press® Publishing Association
Nampa, Idaho
Oshawa, Ontario, Canada
www.pacificpress.com

Cover design by Gerald Lee Monks
Cover design resources from iStockphoto.com
Inside design by Aaron Troia

The author assumes full responsibility for the accuracy of all facts and quotations as cited in this book.

Unless otherwise indicated, Bible references are taken from the New King James Version. Copyright © 1982 by Thomas Nelson, Inc. Used by permission. All rights reserved.

Bible references marked NIV are taken from THE HOLY BIBLE, NEW INTERNATIONAL VERSION®, NIV®. Copyright © 1973, 1978, 1984, 2011 by Biblica, Inc.™ Used by permission. All rights reserved worldwide.

Bible references marked NLT are taken from the Holy Bible, New Living Translation, copyright © 1996, 2004, 2007 by Tyndale House Foundation. Used by permission of Tyndale House Publishers, Inc., Carol Stream, Illinois 60188. All rights reserved.

Bible references marked NASB are from the NEW AMERICAN STANDARD BIBLE®, copyright © 1960, 1962, 1963, 1968, 1971, 1972, 1973, 1975, 1977, 1995 by The Lockman Foundation. Used by permission.

Bible references marked *YLT* are from the 1898 Young's Literal Translation by Robert Young (in the public domain).

Bible references from *The Message*. Copyright © by Eugene H. Peterson, 1993, 1994, 1995, 1996, 2000, 2001, 2002. Used by permission of NavPress Publishing Group.

Bible references marked NRSV are from the New Revised Standard Version Bible, copyright © 1989, Division of Christian Education of the National Council of the Churches of Christ in the United States of America. Used by permission. All rights reserved.

You can obtain additional copies of this book by calling toll-free 1-800-765-6955 or by visiting http://www.adventistbookcenter.com.

Library of Congress Cataloging-in-Publication Data:

Brace, Shawn, 1981-
Pursued : by a relentless God / Shawn Brace.
     p. cm.
ISBN 13: 978-0-8163-2486-6 (pbk.)
ISBN 10: 0-8163-2486-7 (pbk.)
1. God (Christianity) 2. Spirituality. I. Title.
BT103.B725 2011
234—dc23

                                                                              2011021699

11 12 13 14 15 • 5 4 3 2 1

DEDICATION

For Camille, my beautiful bride:
May I learn to pursue you as relentlessly as God does.

TABLE OF CONTENTS

CHAPTER ONE

PURSUED BY GRACE

"The God of the Old Testament," Richard Dawkins writes, "is arguably the most unpleasant character in all fiction: jealous and proud of it; a petty, unjust, unforgiving control-freak; a vindictive, bloodthirsty ethnic cleanser; a misogynistic, homophobic, racist, infanticidal, genocidal, filicidal, pestilential, megalomaniacal, sadomasochistic, capriciously malevolent bully."[1]

God isn't faring very well these days. Dawkins is only one of many outspoken atheists who are doing all they can to destroy belief in Him. Dawkins directs his ire especially at the God of the Old Testament. For many today, the God of the New Testament isn't a whole lot better.

Truth be told, when it comes to God, many of us have reservations. Whether or not we believe in His existence, thoughts of Him raise our anxiety. Just recently, I sat at a small table in a café in a quaint New England town with six or seven young people who are graduate students at an Ivy League school. We get together weekly to discuss a book of choice—and God. On the occasion I'm remembering, a young woman in the group turned red and profanities flew out of her mouth when she spoke of God. She complained, "You Christians think you have all the answers. But this God you serve is messed up."

To say that this woman is angry at God would be an understatement. She's especially upset about the pain and suffering that goes on in the world while this allegedly loving God stands back and does nothing. Of course, we don't have to have such a drastic attitude toward this God to be mistaken about Him. Perhaps we're simply lukewarm about Him. Maybe "playing church" has burned us out. Maybe we're tired of trying to pursue Someone who may or may not be worth the effort. And pursuing Him does take a lot of effort: going to church every week; praying every day; trying to be good. Life is too short and demanding for us to be bothered by these extras. And if this "God" that many religious people—be they Christian, Muslim, Jewish, or Hindu—want to force on us is nothing more than a vindictive control freak, why does He deserve our devotion, adoration, and worship anyway?

But perhaps we're mistaken. Maybe this God is actually anything but vindictive, bloodthirsty, or sadomasochistic. Maybe this God is worth pursuing after all. No, more than that: maybe He's pursuing us.

Christian author Ravi Zacharias shares a story about Alfred E. Smith, former governor of New York and the Democratic nominee for president in 1928. It seems that when Smith and a few friends were on a fishing trip to New England, Smith woke up early one morning to go to church along with a few others of the group. As they tried to sneak past others, they heard one half-awake fellow whisper, "Wouldn't it be awful if it turned out they were right!"[2]

Giving up or rejecting or saying "No thanks" to this God would be a huge mistake, all right—not because He's some kind of exacting being who will unleash all His fury on those who refuse to acknowledge Him, but because that choice would separate us from Someone who wants nothing more than to have intimacy with His creatures.

Looking again . . .

A funny thing happens when one picks up a Bible and turns to the Old Testament. Rather than finding an angry God, one discovers quite the opposite. True, this Testament pictures God acting from His displeasure—which is something that all responsible and loving parents do when their children do things that harm themselves and others. But the heart of this part of Scripture reveals a God who loves. A God who cares. A God who pursues.

Take, for instance, the book of Psalms—a collection of what is considered to be some of the most brilliant poetry in all literature, both secular and sacred. Within that book, Psalm 23, which was written by King David, stands over and above the rest. One person has called this psalm "the pearl of the Psalms, whose soft and pure radiance delights every eye."[3]

It's no wonder that it is described in such terms. Few who read it can resist its splendor—which is evidenced by the fact that it is quoted often, and not only from pulpits but in movies, rock songs, political addresses, and horror novels as well. The imagery in this psalm seems to resonate with everyone. It tugs at the heartstrings of those who can identify with the author. "The LORD is my Shepherd," David writes. "I shall not want."

I spent a year living in Scotland, and more than once I saw there peaceful, tranquil pastoral scenes: green hillsides speckled with white sheep; smoke gently billowing out of the shepherd's stone house. As the shepherds lovingly tended their flocks, I was impressed with the care they gave each of their sheep. While shepherds do have to act tough at times to keep their sheep in line, even that is ultimately for the good of the sheep. That's quite a different picture than a God who is supposedly jealous and angry all the time.

In the six short verses of Psalm 23, David testifies that God cares and provides for His people much like shepherds do for their flocks. This is why David can boldly proclaim that even in the "shadow of death," he will "fear no evil." With the Lord as his Shepherd, he will always find comfort.

The climax of the psalm moves beyond mere creaturely comforts and shepherdlike care. There, David beautifully proclaims that "goodness and mercy"—the very essence of God's character—will "follow" him all the days of his life (verse 6).

Such a thought is overwhelming—to know that God's grace will forever accompany us. David would later testify to this beautiful reality in another psalm, where he proclaimed, "I can never escape from your Spirit! I can never get away from your presence! If I go up to heaven, you are there; if I go down to the place of the dead, you are there. If I ride the wings of the morning, if I dwell by the farthest oceans, even there your hand will guide me, and your strength will support me" (Psalm 139:7–10, NLT).

So, it seemed that no matter what David did or where he went, God never turned His back on him. And, in fact, for all the successes David's story contains, it also is fraught with incredible tragedy and shame. The man who is known for the commitment to defending God's cause and His people against the giant Goliath is the same man who committed adultery with Bathsheba and then had her husband, one of David's best soldiers, killed. David's story does contain many a sad page; many people shed tears because of what he did. Yet through it all, David could confidently write that God stuck by his side. He could confidently maintain that God's goodness and mercy— indeed, His grace—would follow him his entire life.

But there's more to it than that. Unfortunately, when those who translated this psalm into English came to this verse, they robbed it of some of its beauty. This, understandably, happens frequently when people try to translate something from one language to another. In this case, David originally wrote the psalm in Hebrew, and a Hebrew word he used is richer than most of our English versions reveal.

The Hebrew word that David wrote is *radaph*. This word is used more than 140 times in the Old Testament, and time and time again English versions translate it in a particular, meaningful way. But, curiously, when they come to Psalm 23, where the beauty of this word should be on full display, they take a very unfortunate turn. Perhaps because the passage is so well known or perhaps because the King James Version of this psalm is so familiar, they translate the word merely as "follow." However, *radaph* literally means to "chase" or to "pursue." Thus, the translation of Psalm 23:6 should tell us that God's grace doesn't merely "follow" us. No, it—or better yet, He—"pursues" us!

What's the big deal? In my mind, the word *follow* comes infinitely short of God's attitude toward us, what He really does for us. A little dog follows close behind, nipping at our heels as it tries to keep up. A police officer follows from a safe distance in an unmarked car as he tracks a criminal he's been watching. But God's goodness, mercy, love, and grace don't merely follow us all the days of our life. His grace takes a more active, indeed, a more *dynamic* approach. God's grace—God Himself—*pursues* us.

Underwhelmed?

At this point you may be a little underwhelmed. Yet, there is a richness to this reality that we may not appreciate fully at first. The truth is that many people have the mistaken idea that God expects *us* to pursue *Him*. In fact, most religious systems are based on this—which, to a large degree, is a reflection of the fact that many people serve their god out of fear, believing that they must appease their divine master.

Think about it for a second. Some religions, such as Islam, maintain that to attain paradise, a person needs to carry out certain practices. Similarly, Hinduism supposes that in order for people to improve their standing in their next incarnation, known as *samsara,* their karmic account balance must be favorable. People's *karma* determines what they will be reincarnated into in their next cycle of life, as a human being, an animal, an insect, or some other organism. Thus, people's spiritual life is all about trying to make up for the bad things they've done so that in their next reincarnation they can be human beings rather than, for instance, cows.

All these systems of religion are based on the idea that somehow, some way, we, as human beings, can pursue God and His favor, or enlightenment, or paradise, or whatever our goal is. They propose that by following certain steps or abiding by particular rules we can slowly climb the ladder toward eternal peace. Thus, ultimately, the individual person becomes his or her own savior.

Even those who don't believe in God at all aren't immune from life as pursuit. In fact, it's the people who label themselves as atheists or agnostics and want nothing to do with God who are the most likely to be plagued with this do-it-yourself mentality. Atheists' only hope for the future rests upon humankind continually increasing in knowledge and innovation. Stephen Hawking, a British theoretical physicist who is widely regarded as the most brilliant mind of our time, disappointed an audience he was speaking with a few years ago when he announced to them that the human species was in great danger. After passing along this bad news, however, Hawking offered a little hope to his listeners. "If we can keep from destroying each other for the next one hundred years," he said, "sufficient technology will have been developed to distribute humanity to various planets, and then no one tragedy or atrocity will eradicate us all at the same time."[4] The movie *Wall-E* suggested the same thing.

The truth is that the various religions of the world—whether Islam, Buddhism, atheism, or just about any of the others—place the responsibility for humankind's survival and growth directly upon human beings. *They* must pursue God, or knowledge, or whatever is essential to obtaining their salvation.

Unfortunately, many Christians have fallen for such thinking too. They apparently believe that they must pursue God to obtain His favor and His blessings. A woman who attends one of my churches informed me that she wanted to wear a head covering to church because she thought that if she did, God would bless her. She then went on to tell me about all the things she needed to change in her life, using the personal pronoun *I* over and over again. Eventually, I was able to cut her off, and when I did, I challenged her apparent belief that it was her job to pursue God by cleaning up her own life. I pointed out that the Bible, especially the Old Testament, pictures a God who doesn't expect us to pursue Him, but who pursues us— pursues us in love, with only good intentions.

Interestingly, there are numerous places in the Bible in addition to Psalm 23 that use this imagery of a searching Shepherd. In Ezekiel, for instance, God announces, "Indeed, I Myself will search for My sheep and seek them out. As a shepherd seeks out his flock on the day he is among his scattered sheep, so will I seek out My sheep and deliver them from all the places where they were scattered on a cloudy and dark day" (Ezekiel 34:11, 12). In the original Hebrew of the passage, the word *I* is emphasized, indicating that, contrary to the model in which humans pursue God, He has said that He Himself pursues us.

We see this same idea in the New Testament, where Jesus announces His ministry in terms that remind us of this psalm. When some of the religious elite complained that Jesus was partying with prostitutes, sinners, and tax collectors, Jesus turned to them and said, "If a man has a hundred sheep and one of them gets lost, what will he do? Won't he leave the ninety-nine others in the wilderness and go to search for the one that is lost until he finds it?" (Luke 15:4, NLT).

So, the Bible is replete with images of a pursuing Shepherd. Indeed, all of Scripture is firmly established on the reality that God doesn't expect us to pursue Him, to work our way up some ladder to Him. Inherent in that idea—that God expects us to pursue Him—is the concurrent idea that He doesn't think we're worthy of His time, affection, or love. If this were the case, we might as well have a God who is vengeful, jealous, and capricious.

But Scripture portrays a pursuing God—a God who will do all that He can to win the affections of those He created in His image much as a young man pursues a young woman who has stolen his heart. God isn't angry. He is not malevolent. He doesn't stand back with His arms folded across His chest, waiting for us to find Him, waiting for us to climb up to heaven. Instead, He brings heaven down to earth, constantly pursuing His sheep, which have gone astray. Indeed, as we will see, He pursues us so far that He even takes on our flesh and blood.

Such is the truth about the God of the Old Testament, the God of the New Testament—indeed, the God of eternity.

MORE THAN THIS

I sat amazed as I listened to his words. What NFL quarterback Tom Brady said as he was being interviewed on *60 Minutes* probably didn't cause most people to bat an eyelash, but his admission was one of the most sobering revelations I had ever encountered. After talking about his family, about his successes as a professional quarterback, and about his life in general, Brady asked, "Why do I have three Super Bowl rings and still think there's something greater out there for me? I mean maybe a lot of people would say, 'Hey, man, this is what it is. I reached my goal, my dream, my life.' Me, I think: . . . 'It's got to be more than this.' I mean this can't be what it's all cracked up to be."

There it was: the plain, alarming truth. Tom Brady—rich, famous, handsome Tom Brady, who'd won three Super Bowls by his fifth year in professional football—said life has to offer more than this. The admission wouldn't have been so startling if it hadn't come from someone who's supposed to be a prime example of what life is all about.

Brady isn't alone, of course. People the world over have walked down a similar path. They've realized that there has to be more to life than what their dreams have been. Champion tennis player Boris

Becker, for instance, admitted that, unable to deal with the realization that the world's offer of happiness is a mere mirage, he almost committed suicide after winning his second Wimbledon title—the Super Bowl of tennis. "I had no inner peace," he later said. "I was a puppet on a string."[1]

Such admissions might push us common folk toward becoming despondent. After all, if the rich and famous—with their beauty, fortune, and talent—can't find fulfillment, what hope is there for us who may be a few pounds heavier and a few dollars poorer and who don't have any delusions about the possibility of our achieving the type of success they have?

If all of us were to be honest with ourselves, we might have to admit that many of the things we believed would bring us fulfillment actually left us feeling empty. We've found over and over again that the saying "all that glitters is not gold" is startlingly true. And it's embarrassingly true that we can even get conned into thinking that it's the little stuff that will really give us satisfaction.

I enjoy photography as a hobby, and I don't know how many times I've found myself yearning for a new lens for my camera. I don't want a two-thousand-dollar lens. I don't necessarily want five lenses. I just want that one lens that I know will improve my photography tenfold. Of course, when I get that lens, I enjoy it for a while, only to find myself yearning for another lens that will, no doubt, put my photography over the top.

Such is the cycle of life. We keep setting our hopes on that "something" that seems to promise fulfillment. But when we obtain the object, win the championship, secure the job promotion, the question "Now what?" keeps ringing in our ears. As Christian author Ravi Zacharias observes, "Surely, the loneliest moment in life is when you have just experienced what you thought would deliver the ultimate, and it has let you down."[2]

Some of us like to believe that human relationships are the answer. Instead of placing our money and energies on material things, we invest our resources in human beings. To be sure, this is a noble pursuit. Relationships really are the stuff of life. And yet they can take us only so far. No one lives forever. Unfortunately, love is often spurned. And often, the feelings we've had for that special someone fizzle out, or their feelings for us do. Psychologists have discovered that the "in love" feeling—what some label "romantic obsession"—that people experience when they think about that special someone lasts, on average, two years.[3] It's no wonder, then, that the typical Hollywood marriage lasts about as long as it takes to say "I do." And yet these are the people who have been ordained to tell us both on the screen and in song what love looks like.

Thus, we are all left thirsting, we are all left longing, for something that truly satisfies.

"Everything is meaningless"

Toward the end of his life the wise man Solomon came to some surprising conclusions. Solomon was the second child that Bathsheba bore David, and he seemed to inherit some of his father's bad traits. After ascending to the throne upon his father's death, he enjoyed what most people would deem great success. He became incredibly wealthy and obtained seven hundred wives, not to mention scores of mistresses. All should have seemed right in Solomon's world. Yet, all was not right. He eventually realized that those things he thought would bring him satisfaction left him feeling empty. This led him to introduce and conclude his book Ecclesiastes with the words, "Everything is meaningless . . . utterly meaningless!" (Ecclesiastes 1:2; 12:8, NLT). But he didn't leave it at that. His experience had allowed him to come to the realization that what his heart had yearned for was right there in front of him. It was the same yearning that his father had; the same yearning that his ancestors Abraham, Isaac, and Jacob had. Thus, Solomon proclaimed that God "has planted eternity in the human heart" (Ecclesiastes 3:11, NLT).

In other words, the God of this universe has placed within every human heart the yearning for eternity, the yearning for "forever," as the Hebrew literally says—the yearning for something transcendent, for something outside ourselves. We have within us a longing for that which only God—the One who owns eternity—can give. Some have described this yearning as a "God-shaped hole." I like to look at it as a "grace-shaped hole," reflecting the reality that deep down inside, all of us want to be pursued by God and His grace.

Unfortunately, too many times we try to shove other things into that grace-shaped hole, much like trying to put a square peg into a round hole. Instead of allowing God's eternity—His love, His grace, His "forever"—to fill that void in our hearts, we try to fill it with the here and now. We try to fill it with temporary things—things that don't last forever.

Of course, this is not to say that these things are necessarily bad in and of themselves. Money, per se, isn't bad. Nor are possessions or human relationships. But when we make these things an end unto themselves, we run the risk of trying to reduce eternity to the threescore and ten years we are on this earth.

Christian apologist C. S. Lewis expressed this idea beautifully. Lewis was himself an atheist for a number of years. When he eventually discovered the joys of Christianity, influenced in part by J. R. R. Tolkien of *The Lord of the Rings* fame, he became an ardent promoter of the Christian faith. In his classic work *Mere Christianity*, Lewis hints at the idea that he was searching for eternity during much of his life, and ultimately found it in the God of Christianity. " 'Creatures are not born with desires,' " he wrote, " 'unless satisfaction for those desires exists. A baby feels hunger: well, there is such a thing as food. A duckling wants to swim: well, there is such a thing as water. Men feel sexual desire: well, there is such a thing as sex. If I find in myself a desire which no experience in this world can satisfy, the most probable explanation is that I was made for another world.' "[4]

No doubt, many of us can identify with Lewis. There are many wonderful things in this world that satisfy our temporal desires. But even after we take care of our needs and then address these desires, an uneasiness tugs at our hearts and makes us feel empty. This is because God has placed within us a longing for eternity, and we won't find true and lasting satisfaction until we recognize and surrender to this longing.

Addressing God, Augustine, who lived sixteen hundred years ago, wrote, "Thou hast made us for Thyself, and our hearts are restless till they rest in Thee." In other words, just as Solomon, C. S. Lewis, and every other honest person since has recognized, our lives are incredibly empty and unfulfilled until we respond to the grace that the pursuing God brings to us. Until then, we will continue to chase after temporary fixes and fleeting ecstasies that cannot satisfy us for long.

The living water

The New Testament book of John shares a story on this matter. On His way from Judea to Galilee, Jesus stops in Samaria. Normally, when Jews of Jesus' day traveled between Galilee and Judea, they would detour around Samaria, even though the most direct route went through that district. The Jews went miles out of their way because they despised the Samaritans and wanted to avoid them at all costs. But John tells us Jesus "needed to go through Samaria" (John 4:4).

Extremely thirsty, Jesus sits down next to a well, and when a Samaritan woman comes to draw water from the well, He asks her for a drink. The woman is shocked. Not only is Jesus a Jew and she a Samaritan, but she is a woman, and in those days, men didn't talk to women in public. In fact, many Jewish men began their days with a prayer thanking God that they were neither Gentiles, slaves, nor women. So for Jesus to talk to a Samaritan woman is extremely daring and puzzling.

After the woman gets over her initial shock, it soon becomes apparent that she is the one who is truly in need of water—but not the kind of water that fills a well or flows from a faucet. The kind of water she needs is living water, eternal water—water that only God can provide.

Jesus tells this woman to go get her husband. Her nerves sparking, she replies, "I have no husband" (verse 17).

She really doesn't have a husband. She's had five husbands, Jesus points out, but she isn't married to the man she is living with now. From our perspective, then, we can surmise that over the course of her beleaguered life she has become involved with six different men, hoping that one of them would give her satisfaction—but none were able to provide what she really needed. Little did she know that the seventh guy she would meet would be the One to finally fulfill the longings of her heart. This Guy took a different route to Galilee than normal so He could pursue her with His grace.

I can just imagine the emptiness this woman must have felt prior to this encounter with Jesus. She had spent her whole life pursuing love, pursuing grace, pursuing fulfillment. She had been married five times, each time hoping she had finally found her knight in shining armor. Each time, however, she had met with incredible disappointment, so, instead of sticking it out with the one she was married to, she had moved on to another man, hoping against all hope that with this one the feelings of ecstasy would never end. And when that didn't work, she wondered if perhaps simply living together with Knight in Shining Armor Number Six would do the trick—as if the "I dos" were for some reason souring things.

I'm sure many of us can identify with this woman. Maybe we haven't been married five times. Maybe instead we've sought satisfaction five times in buying new cars while the ones we were driving were still in good shape. Or maybe we've made five jumps from job to job, or taken five vacation trips halfway around the world, only to finally realize that no place in this world can truly satisfy us.

To us, as to the Samaritan woman, Jesus of Nazareth proclaims, "Whoever drinks of the water that I shall give him will never thirst" (verse 14). John tells us that when the Samaritan woman tastes this water, when she finally realizes that this Man Jesus is the piece that fits into the grace-shaped hole in her heart, she leaves her water pot at the well, goes into her city, and invites everyone she sees to "come, see a Man who told me all things that I ever did," asking, "Could this be the Christ?" (verse 29).

It's as if she thinks it too good to be true. She almost can't believe her good fortune. A "chance" meeting at a well has turned her life around. She's spent her whole existence searching for a man who would pursue and satisfy her, and now she wonders, "Could this be the Man?" She's pursued love many times, only to be burned each time. Now the ultimate love has come in pursuit of her.

The God who pursued the Samaritan woman pursues us too. He longs to fill the grace-shaped hole that we all have. He longs to let us know that He is the fulfillment of all we ever dreamed of. And He wants nothing less than to impress us with the reality that He has created us for another world. There's more to life than an endless, meaningless cycle. There is a way out. God is pursuing us, and He will place Himself in our grace-shaped holes if we will just allow Him to.

The pursuing God

In his book *The Search for God at Harvard,* Ari Goldman shares an interesting story about one of his classmates at Harvard Divinity School who found the truth about his grace-shaped hole. It didn't come easily, however. Robert had been a successful developer and the CEO of a thirty-two-million dollar company in the Boston area. Unfortunately, the company went belly up, and he had to file for bankruptcy.

And then the wheels really fell off. During the three years after Robert lost the company, his father and his father-in-law passed away, his wife became an alcoholic, and his oldest child was hospitalized for a year. Robert soon realized that all the things he had placed his trust, hope, and faith in were ephemeral. But then things turned around. He told Goldman, "One day I was on my way home and could barely drive the car. I got out of the car and got down on my knees and prayed for help. I had hit bottom. I admitted absolute and total defeat. I prayed for help not believing that anybody could help me. But when I got up, I knew something extraordinary had happened. For the first time, there was a clarity, a lightness, a sense of peace."[5]

He was soon able to identify where that peace came from. It came from God. And Robert began going to church regularly and reading his Bible. "I read the Scriptures, mostly the psalms," he says, "and found they had a meaning I never saw before."[6]

What happened to Robert is no mystery. Like so many others, he had finally realized that the things we so often pursue in life—fortune, fame, and even family—can't fill that grace-shaped hole that only God and His pursuing grace can fill.

Those things can't fill the hole in our heart either. Only God can, and He is eager to do just that. Will you allow Him to? Will you finally surrender to the fact that only God can truly satisfy?

CHAPTER THREE

THE DIVINE MOTIVE

William Seward is one of the most underrated persons in United States history.* This politician from New York, who was once the foremost figure in the Republican Party, was overshadowed by a much more celebrated contemporary of his: Abraham Lincoln.

In 1860, Seward was the frontrunner for the Republican nomination for president. Most people thought that he was a shoo-in for the presidency, so it came as a surprise when Lincoln—who, for much of the primary season, was actually third or fourth in the race—came out on top. Shrewd politician that he was, Lincoln invited his chief rivals to serve as members of his cabinet. Seward became his secretary of state and soon was his most trusted confidant.

And that was for good reason. Seward was a brilliant politician and a wonderful human being. He was actually a more zealous opponent of slavery than Lincoln was. In one instance, a black man named William Freeman brutally murdered a man and his wife and small child. When the authorities caught him, Freeman confessed gleefully. As he was hauled to jail, an angry mob nearly lynched him. Finally, when he was brought to court and his trial was opened, no

---

*Though you can buy T-shirts that say "I Love William Seward"!

lawyer dared represent him; the citizens of the city threatened violence against anyone who would take his case.

When the judge asked if there was anyone who would defend Freeman, silence enveloped the courtroom. Finally, Seward said emotionally, "May it please the court, *I shall remain counsel for the prisoner until his death!*"[1] This was the kind of man Seward was.

Despite his tender heart and admirable principles, however, Seward had his flaws. One major flaw was his ambition. Early in his career especially, his political aspirations seemed to overshadow his love for his wife, Frances. This ultimately resulted in Frances's developing an unhealthy attachment to one of Seward's political allies. When Seward was away from home, Frances would spend a lot of time with this other man. But before a romantic affair commenced, Frances came to her senses and told her husband of the relationship. She desperately wanted him to confront the man about the situation, but Seward, not wanting to alienate a political ally, never got around to it.

While campaigning in upstate New York, Seward finally recognized that his ambitions had damaged his relationship with his wife, and he wrote a penitent letter to her, pleading for forgiveness. When a few months passed and he still had no response from Frances, Seward anxiously wrote her another letter, expressing his hope that their relationship wasn't beyond repair. Frances responded, writing that he was being too hard on himself and that she had in fact forgiven him. She said that she never doubted that he was a "good and kind" man, and then she quoted a sentence written by a popular women's author of the time, a sentence that put into words the dilemma they were in: " 'Love is the whole history of woman and but an episode in the life of man.' "[2]

Frances recognized something that very few of us seem to understand, something that is missing from most of Hollywood's love stories: Even great men fail at love. Of course, it need not be so, but all too often it is: while a woman's heart may be tightly chained to her man, the reverse may not be true. Certainly the Samaritan woman whom Jesus talked with at the well found this out a few too many times.

Over and over again, "love" that was hot and heavy at the beginning of a relationship fizzles out as things progress. This is especially true of men who consider romance a chase and who have caught their "prey." Having done so, they want to move on to their next victory, their next achievement, their next conquest.

To be fair to men, women can do the same. Unless something supernatural happens to our hearts, both men and women will consider love to be simply an episode in their lives. Though Hollywood may promise us eternal romantic bliss, too many people have found out the hard way that "happily ever after" rarely lasts longer than it takes to roll the credits.

But this isn't a book of relational advice. I raise this point simply to draw a contrast between the fragile, ephemeral nature of the love that we human beings—even the best of us—have and what the Bible says about the love that God has. Perhaps the most revealing passage is in one of the last books of the Bible. It names the very essence of God. John offers this insight twice in his first epistle. He writes, "God is love" (1 John 4:8, 16). Just those three words: *God . . . is . . . love.*

Simple though it is, however, this statement is a bit puzzling. Were we given the opportunity to describe God, to tell what He is all about, very few of us would say merely that He is love. *Powerful* maybe. *All-wise* perhaps. But *love*? The word seems inadequate— rather underwhelming when used in reference to the One who runs the universe. We would rather the biblical authors use words that bring up images of power and control to describe God. Love seems too weak—too much like something fitting for a little puppy that cries for its master to return home.

Notice, too, that John doesn't say God is "loving," or that He "loves." Such formulations would describe what God is like, or what He does, but they wouldn't describe *who He is.* Human beings can love, but we cannot be defined as love. In John's declaration, the word *love* is a noun. Saying "God is love," then, is akin to saying, "John F. Kennedy is fire," or "Winston Churchill is rock." These things don't make sense.

But love, the "substance," is the very essence of God's character. It is who He is, what He does, why He acts. It is His *raison d'être*, and we must conclude that everything He does stems from this supreme principle. Indeed, love is His prime motivation.

Of course, we need to qualify this idea. The simple statement that God is love requires further exploration because, truthfully, the idea that God is love doesn't sit well with us if it's the variety of love that's so frequently portrayed in movies and pop songs. That brand of love seems to be fleeting and self-serving.

And then there are the other nuances of love. Many of us can say "I love you" to our spouse or other family members and then turn around and say "I love ice cream" the next minute. What does that mean? Can the attitude and affection we have toward our family be expressed by the same word that we use to tell how we feel about food or our possessions or television shows? As one of my friends has pointed out in a book she's written, "We use one word for love that is Holy and the same word for love that is wholly Hollywood."[3] That's why the Bible's declaration that God is love leaves us scratching our heads a bit—if God is going to pursue us with His love, we want to know what type of love is motivating Him.

Love defined

Fortunately, when John tells us that God is love, he has a very specific flavor of love in mind. As we saw in chapter 1 of this book, we English speakers are very limited when it comes to the word *love;* we use the same word in a variety of situations. However, though in English we have to use just one word for all of love's many nuances, the Greek language—the language that John and the rest of the New Testament authors used—has four different words.

When New Testament authors, John included, referred to God and His love, they used the word *agapē*. Perhaps you've heard this word before. It stands in contrast to the other words for love that people writing in Greek had in their arsenal. Perhaps the most well-known of those other words is *eros*, from which we get the word *erotic.* This type of love was closely related to the Greek god known as Eros, whose Roman counterpart was Cupid—that cute little guy we often see around Valentine's Day armed with a bow and arrows. The imagery suggests that erotic love can't be controlled. People hit by Cupid's "love arrows" inevitably have to satisfy the lust with which those arrows infect their targets.

Truth be told, this is what many of us today think when we discuss what love is. This is the kind of love people have in mind when they talk about "falling in love" upon meeting a person and then "falling out of love" just as quickly. Eros/Cupid's arrows have made them his captives and left them unable to resist the pull of erotic love. And once that love has been quenched, Eros pulls his arrow out, and, *abracadabra,* they mysteriously fall in love with the next person whom they find attractive.

God's love has nothing in common with this kind of love, and anyone who tells you that a bit of erotic love is necessary for one to have a vibrant sex life with one's spouse hasn't read the biblical witness. The Bible doesn't tell husbands to love their wives with erotic love, nor does it say that God's love is erotic.* If there is one word that could be used in place of *eros,* it's the word *selfish.* Erotic love is selfish. When a guy walks down the street and finds himself wishing he could jump into bed with the hot blonde walking in his direction, he isn't thinking about her needs; he's thinking about his carnal, lustful desires. When two little girls fight over the last cookie on the plate, they're motivated by their self-centered desire for gratification rather than by selfless love. Both the guy walking down the street and the little girls fighting over the cookie are engaging in a little bit of erotic "love," and the Bible associates nothing of the sort with God.

What does the Bible mean when it tells us that God is *agapē*—a word that Carsten Johnsen calls the "term par excellence" of the

---

*Interestingly, the Greek translations of the Song of Solomon—a book of the Bible written by King Solomon that deals extensively with love and sex—never uses the word *eros.* This is somewhat surprising to the many who have considered this book to be a representation of erotic love, which they think is normative and necessary between husband and wife.

Christian faith?[4] Whereas *eros* is all about acting out of self-interest, *agapē* acts in the interests of others. And this is precisely what God does. He *never* acts out of self-interest. God is always looking for ways to give of Himself rather than to take for Himself. As John says earlier in his epistle, "This is how we know what love is: Jesus Christ laid down his life for us" (1 John 3:16, NIV). In other words, if a person wants to know what the definition of love is, He can look to Jesus, who emptied Himself completely for the well-being of human-kind. This is the essence of *agapē* love. God gives and gives and gives—to the point of even giving His life for humanity.

The queen of the Methodists

Hannah More seems to have understood this. She was a British playwright and philanthropist who befriended William Wilberforce—that great politician who was the catalyst in the abolition of slavery in nineteenth-century England. More was an abolitionist as well. She also wrote extensively on education, ethics, and theology, outselling Jane Austen in her day, and she was later known as the "Queen of the Methodists." She gave one of the best explanations of this magnifi-cent force called love when she wrote, "Love never reasons, but pro-fusely gives; it gives like a thoughtless prodigal its all, and then trem-bles lest it has done too little."[5]

Could it be that this is a description of God's very essence—He profusely gives like a thoughtless prodigal and then stays up all night, worrying He has not given enough? This seems to be what John says about God, and these sentiments are certainly echoed in other bibli-cal passages as well. The apostle Paul, for example, repeats this idea when he writes to the Roman believers that "God demonstrates his own love for us in this: While we were still sinners, Christ died for us" (Romans 5:8, NIV). People who give their lives for others have given all they can, and as we will see later, this is the measurement of what God has given. It's the measure of how much He loves us.

It is a bit of a mystery why God acts as He does. Why does God cause the "sun to rise on the evil and the good, and [send] rain on the righteous and the unrighteous" (Matthew 5:45, NIV)? Such actions are certainly contrary to our human inclinations. We tend to act nicely only to those who can do something for us, those who can give us something in return. God isn't like that. We humans often turn our backs on those who have stopped being useful to us; but God lavishes His love upon the outcasts.

Some propose that God's love defies logic, as if He loves us for no reason at all. They would have us think that God loves for the simple fact that He is love and that we have no value to Him whatsoever. This is supposed to make God's love all the more admirable, yet it does just the opposite. The truth is that the reason God loves us need not really be a mystery. Carsten Johnsen sums it up perfectly.

> We, all of us, constantly tended to forget the tremendous historical fact that man was created by God, in His image. *Therefore*, and obviously for no other "more important" reason, we have also constantly failed to see why he could love us and still remain perfectly intelligent. After all, he had some realistic foundation to base His love on.
>
> The fact that man is God's own creature is reason enough for Him to love that man. In fact, it is not only an intelligent reason. It is an absolutely inevitable reason. As long as creation is a fact—and I do not see who could manage to change it into a non-fact; for even God cannot reverse history, or make done things undone—*you* are the Creator's creature. You yourself could not, even with the most obstinate efforts of your will power, move one single inch from the unshakeable fact that He is your Maker, the Generator of your life, the constant Upholder of your existence.[6]

This is the reality of God's love. Because He has created us, "fathered" us, He will never stop loving us or providing for us. As Johnsen says, we can try to do all that we can to change the fact that we were created by God, but we will never be able to change history.

Thus, we will never be able to free ourselves from God's love. As the great English writer G. K. Chesterton reminds us, "Love is not blind; that is the last thing it is. Love is bound."[7] God's love is bound tightly to us in a way that can never be amended. Just as ideal parents never stop loving their children no matter what happens precisely because they created those children and brought them into the world; so God loves us because He created us and brought us into this world. This is reason enough for Him to shower us prodigiously with His love.

This is also why God said, through the prophet Jeremiah, "I have loved you with an everlasting love" (Jeremiah 31:3, NIV). His love for us has existed from eternity past because He is everlasting and therefore His love is everlasting. Indeed, long before you were born, God anticipated your existence and already had an infinite love for you—much like soon-to-be parents eagerly anticipate the arrival of their child. Like those parents, God ever seeks to provide for us; He ever seeks to have His sun shine on us, whether we are good, bad, or somewhere in between.

Some may find God's love hard to understand because they didn't have parents who treated them in this way. They didn't experience everlasting love that sticks with us through thick and thin. For them to understand God's love, they have to overcome some unfortunate and unnatural circumstances. But it can be done. When we surrender ourselves to this pursuing God, He so overwhelms us with His *agapē* love that our value and potential reach heights we never would have thought possible—all because God is love, a love that according to Paul "never fails" (1 Corinthians 13:8).

"Useless" Jim

For about fifteen years, Jim was the food service director at the nursing home where my mother works in the Boston area.[8] Then, in 2006, he was diagnosed with cancer. Though he tried to work for a while after his diagnosis, ultimately his employer had to let him go because the cancer had so debilitated him that he was of no use to the nursing home anymore. However, for the whole next year, though

Jim's time was divided between sitting at home and going to the hospital for treatment and he didn't do a lick of work for the nursing home, his former employer continued to pay him his full salary.

In October of that year, Jim got a personal phone call from one of the owners of the nursing home system—a man who had dozens of nursing home and assisted living facilities across Massachusetts and almost two thousand employees. This man said, "A limousine is going to pick you up at your house tonight at five o'clock. Be ready. I have two tickets for Game 1 of the World Series at Fenway Park, and you're going to be my honored guest."

So there was Jim—"useless," cancer-filled Jim, a lifelong Red Sox fan—enjoying a full-time salary that he didn't deserve and sitting in Fenway Park to watch the first game of major league baseball's World Series. And next to him was a man who, though probably not a follower of Christ, displayed the same love that defines God's very essence.

Yet as good as that man's deed was, it bore but a faint reflection of the love of the God of the universe, whose every action is soaked in the motive of love—a love that is forever bound to the beings He created.

We all come from different backgrounds, and we all have different baggage. But deep down inside, we're all yearning for that kind of everlasting, unfailing, never-ending love. And the beautiful thing about all this is that God is directing this unfailing love toward *you*!

How can you, how can I, not respond to a love like that?

CHAPTER FOUR

FREE AGENTS

It's funny how things work out. One of the best-kept secrets in science is that Charles Darwin—the godfather of modern science—first formulated his theories on the origins of life based upon an assumption about God. In fact, far from being a purely scientific theory, Darwin's evolutionary paradigm was mostly a theological one. And we can't really blame him. At some point, every thinking person has to figure out what he or she is going to do with God—especially when there's a clash between one's understanding of God and one's understanding of the world.

In 1860, after the publication of his master treatise, *On the Origin of Species,* good ol' Chuck wrote a letter in which he tried to justify his theory to a friend. He didn't use purely empirical and scientific means to explain himself. Instead, he candidly admitted, "There seems to me too much misery in the world." This statement isn't all that profound. But what he said next is perhaps as profound as it is simple—especially since most of us, if we were to be honest with ourselves—have thought something similar. "I cannot persuade myself," Darwin wrote, "that a beneficent and omnipotent God would have designedly created the [parasitic wasp] with the express intention of their feeding within the living bodies of Caterpillars, or that a cat should play with mice."[1]

You see, Darwin had a dilemma: He had been told his whole life—both in his upbringing and during his clerical training—that God was not only all-powerful and all-knowing, but also all-loving. So, Darwin couldn't help wondering why this all-loving and all-powerful God designed a world that included what he called the "cruel works of nature,"[2] of beast preying upon beast.

As I said, we can't blame Darwin for asking the question. Most of us have wondered about it too at some point in our lives. It isn't a new question. In fact, it's a very old one. The Greek philosopher Epicurus posed what is now known as the "Epicurean paradox" three hundred years before Christ walked on this earth. He put it this way: "Either God wants to abolish evil, and cannot; or he can, but does not want to. If he wants to, but cannot, he is impotent. If he can, but does not want to, he is wicked. If God can abolish evil, and God really wants to do it, why is there evil in the world?"[3] His love would compel Him to oppose such things, and His power would enable Him to overcome them.

Of course, you and I have experienced pain ourselves. Romantic overtures are spurned. Jobs are lost. Loved ones pass away. All this happens to us in the here and now, so we don't need a dead philosopher—or a dead scientist, for that matter—to tell us about it. No matter what we call it or who thought of it first, our hearts continue to be overwhelmed by the apparent contradiction between God's love and our pain, and we want answers.

Before we continue exploring this important topic, I want to share a small, yet important, caveat. That is, I have to admit that I have lived my entire life without encountering a great deal of pain. Yes, I've had brushes with rejection, injury, and death, but nothing serious enough to qualify me to write authoritatively on the subject. So I don't pretend to be writing from great experience. I can't claim to know what people who have experienced pain to the nth degree have gone through.

But, though I would never try to offer some deep philosophical answer to this great question when I'm visiting people who are on their deathbeds, I think that when we can lay aside the emotions that pain produces, we can make sense of it. In fact, I believe that not only can we make sense of it, but when we finally discover the wonderful truth about how God relates to the pain that plagues this world, our hearts will actually be drawn closer to Him.

Father knows best

Not long ago I became a father. I have to admit that before I experienced it, I had heard so much about how amazing the adventure was that I was convinced it wouldn't be able to match the hype. Was I ever wrong! I love looking down into my son Camden's beautiful blue eyes and seeing the smile on his face. I have the privilege of caring for him in the mornings as my wife, Camille, works for a few hours each day, and I feel blessed to be able just to walk into his bedroom after he has awakened and look over the side of his crib to see his smiling face. Priceless!

Of course, being a father isn't a cakewalk by any stretch of the imagination. There are the dirty diapers that never seem to end—you know, dirty diapers that wives enjoy having their husbands change. (Gone are the days when men simply worked outside the home and expected their wives to take care of everything related to the kids!) There are the times when Camden doesn't want to eat no matter what I place in front of him. And of course there's the greatest nuisance of them all: the 3:00 A.M. crying sessions that last for an hour or two and end all hope for a good night's sleep.

So far, this matter of loss of sleep is the only issue that has caused me to lose my cool. A month or two after Camden was born, we all went to Maine, where I had some meetings to attend. Usually, I'm essentially in charge of my schedule and can sleep in a bit on the mornings Camden keeps me up half the night, but that wasn't an option in this case—and it seems to me that the little devil knew it! Well, probably not; but he woke up every thirty or forty minutes through the whole night to voice his dissatisfaction with having to sleep in a foreign crib, in a foreign house, in a foreign state.

Unfortunately, since Camille and I are new parents, though I'm not sure professionals would have had better luck, we knew of nothing we could do to calm him down. So, after a couple of nights of sleeplessness, I was extremely tired and lost my cool. In no uncertain terms, I let poor Camden know that what he was doing was completely unacceptable. Almost as soon as I stopped yelling, an incredible sense of disappointment that I had lost my cool with him overwhelmed me, and I've never since allowed myself to become as frustrated.

These experiences with Camden have led me to two conclusions: first, since he is only thirteen months old as of this writing, I'm sure things will only get harder. And second, I've come to realize that I wouldn't have it any other way.

The truth is that I would rather have a child who can refuse to do exactly what I want him to do than one who can't. Admittedly, there are some nights when I wish that we could simply press a button as we put Camden to bed, and, like a robot, he would sleep through the night. And there are times when I wish he wouldn't run away from me when I'm trying to give him a bath. But all in all, one of the most fulfilling aspects of any relationship—whether it is husband-wife, parent-child, or some other relationship—is knowing that the other person has chosen to be in that relationship; that he or she has decided on his or her own to respect your wishes.

When God set out to create human beings, He had to decide between freely chosen relationships and automated conformity. He could easily have created beings who toed the line no matter what. He could have created a thousand Camdens who couldn't run away or cry all night or disobey. He could have created an entire population who, every day, automatically say, "Good morning, God. I love You. What do You want me to do for You today?" But how fulfilling would that be? Would it be *love*?

Hardly.

Here's where Charles Darwin was sadly misled. Many other well-meaning thinkers, and even Christians, have been misled here as well. They look at the world and assume that things are *exactly* as God wants them to be. They know He's all-powerful, so they reason that means He must exercise His power in all things. When a lion preys upon a zebra, God must have orchestrated the event. When a father beats his child, God must have wanted it to happen. But this concept does *not* match what the Bible teaches, nor does it stand up to simple logic.

When God ran

The Gospel of Luke contains a parable Jesus told about a father who knew much more heartache than I have yet known. "A man had two sons," Jesus said. "The younger son told his father, 'I want my share of your estate now before you die' " (Luke 15:11, 12, NLT). In our culture we have a little inkling of just how bold this son's request was, but it's nothing compared to how shocked Jesus' audience in that time and place would have been.

To begin with, a younger son's asking for his inheritance *before* his father died was mind-boggling. It was more than a mere slap in the face—it was the epitome of disrespect. The son was essentially declaring to his father that he considered him to be dead.

Yet before Jesus' audience had gotten over their shock at that part of the story, Jesus threw another log on the fire. He said, "So his father agreed to divide his wealth between his sons." This was simply unheard of. In essence, the father was allowing his son to call the shots. He was allowing him to control the situation and make the decisions. The father humbled himself deeply to give his son that freedom.

The next verse piles the fuel even higher. Jesus says, "A few days later this younger son packed all his belongings and moved to a distant land, and there he wasted all his money in wild living" (verse 13). Now, let's be clear about this: the father in this story no more wanted his son to take his inheritance prematurely, leave home with it, and waste it, than our heavenly Father wants us to disobey Him.

Jesus' parable is a precise depiction of the divine dilemma. God could either program automated obedience or He could allow free-dom, which must come accompanied by the risk of rejection.

Both fathers—the one in the parable and the One in heaven—chose freedom. God did so because He values freedom more than about any other principle in the whole universe. He would rather give us the power to choose than make us robots because, as we have hinted before, He is a relational Being, and love cannot exist without freedom; it cannot exist where one has no choice but to obey. And whenever people are given freedom—*true* freedom—there is always a possibility that they will reject the One who has made them free.

And this is precisely what happened to the father in Jesus' parable: his son rejected him. No doubt he felt incredibly sad. No doubt he had doubts, wondering whether he had done the right thing. But then he began doing what any loving father would do: he went out to the end of the driveway every night to see if his son was coming home. He checked his e-mail every ten minutes to see if maybe, just maybe, his son had sent him a message, saying he wanted to return.

Then one night it happens. There's an almost indiscernible figure on the horizon. As the person draws closer, the father is able to make out his features more clearly. It's his son! He's returned home! Over-whelmed with excitement and joy, the father starts running full bore toward his son—in that culture, something distinguished men didn't do. When he reaches him, he doesn't begin with formalities or pleas-antries. Instead, he throws his arms around his son and weeps uncon-trollably. Freedom has brought his son home!

Even though I'm just beginning as a father, I know that that fa-ther's run was all the sweeter because he was going to embrace a son who had chosen to be embraced. Love could truly be enjoyed be-cause it was freely given. That it had been rejected only made its re-turn that much more appreciated.

Power isn't control

You see, it's true that God is all-powerful, but there are a few things we need to understand about power. In the first place, power isn't the same as control. In fact, power can be the polar opposite of control. Often, it's the person who doesn't have much power who tries to assert control, who tries to micromanage everyone else. No one wants to be around or have a relationship with that kind of person, and any obedience offered them is mere outward compliance. The actions may be there, but the heart is far removed.

So, we make a dire mistake when we imply that God controls everything that happens in the universe. Now, don't get me wrong; if God so chose, He could control everything and everyone. But such behavior wouldn't get what God wants: a free-flowing, reciprocal love-relationship with His creatures. As Swiss theologian Emil Brunner said, God "is the One who wills to have from me a free response to His love, a response which gives back love for love, a living echo, a living reflection of His glory."[4] Thus, it wouldn't be very impressive, at least in my book, if God took His creatures and announced to the universe, "See My power—I was able to take these robots and make them do what I wanted them to do!" I'm not sure who would be impressed. Certainly not God Himself.

It seems to me that *true* power is displayed in a person's ability to capture someone else's commitment when that other person has the freedom to do otherwise. This is why God told the prophet Zechariah long ago, " 'Not by might, nor by power, but by My Spirit,' says the LORD" (Zechariah 4:6). That is, this all-powerful, almighty God doesn't try to overpower His creatures in an attempt to get them to respond or obey. To put it bluntly and crudely, that's more like rape than love. Instead, God, the constant gentleman, uses His Spirit to pursue, draw, invite, and win over the hearts and allegiance of His creatures. But the whole time He honors our freedom—which allows people to reject Him and what He has to offer.

This is precisely what happened in Old Testament times when the children of Israel said they wanted a king. The prophet Samuel felt that they didn't appreciate him and were casting him off when they insisted upon the change. But the Lord sadly told him, "They have not rejected you, but they have rejected Me, that I should not reign over them" (1 Samuel 8:7). Over and over again through both the Old and New Testaments we see this same attitude in the hearts of those God longs to have a relationship with. And even though God's ultimate desire is for "everyone to be saved" (1 Timothy 2:4, NLT) and come into a relationship with Him, this simply won't be the reality in the end. Many have rejected Him and will continue to do so no matter how lovingly He pursues them.

I wish Charles Darwin had understood this. His confusion led him to formulate a theory that he thought got God off the hook, but that theory ultimately led him to reject God altogether. Ironically, the very thing that Darwin found so deplorable is what shows us that God is desperately seeking a relationship with us. Yes, the world could be perfectly beautiful and safe—free from heartache and pain. But if that came at the expense of freedom and the ability to have a true, loving relationship with our Creator, I'm not sure it would be a world worth living in. I'm certain God doesn't think so.

CHAPTER FIVE

GRACE REJECTED

The late Malcolm Muggeridge, who was an English satirist turned Christian, once shared a sobering experience he had while working as a journalist in India. One warm evening he decided to cool off in a nearby river. Much to his utter surprise and delight, as he entered the refreshing waters, he noticed that an Indian woman had come to the other side of the river to take a bath. "She took off her clothes and stood naked," he recounted, "her brown body just caught by the sun."

Passion quickly had its way, and with little hesitation, Muggeridge—who was married at the time but had always struggled tremendously with lustful temptation—dived into the water and darted as fast as he could swim toward her, envisioning the blissful encounter he imagined surely awaited him on the other side of the river. His fantasies were quickly dashed, however, when he came up out of the water. The woman in front of him, he said, "was old and hideous, and her feet were deformed and turned inwards and her skin was wrinkled, and worst of all, she was a leper."[1]

Muggeridge retreated quickly, muttering to himself about the woman's impropriety and incredible lechery. But then he realized it wasn't the woman who was to be blamed, but he himself. *He* was the one who had acted out of lust, the one whose heart was ruled by unbridled passion, and he realized his grave sinfulness.

No doubt we have all had similar experiences. Sometimes, though, the temptations that come to us don't slap us in the face as quickly as Muggeridge's did. And sometimes the woman on the other side actually is beautiful, and so we imbibe. However, though we may feel a momentary satisfaction, it's as inevitable as the rising of the sun that the waters that at first tasted sweet will become bitter.

Wise King Solomon has some very appropriate insight for us on this subject: "The lips of an immoral woman are as sweet as honey, and her mouth is smoother than oil," he once wrote to his son. But, he cautioned, "in the end she is as bitter as poison, as dangerous as a double-edged sword. Her feet go down to death; her steps lead straight to the grave" (Proverbs 5:3–5, NLT). In light of this, he counsels, "drink water from your own cistern, and running water from your own well" (verse 15, NKJV).

Of course, even though in this particular context Solomon was speaking about sexual temptations, the idea encompasses much more than that. Whether we are drinking from the wells of someone else's spouse (whether in actuality or in fantasy) or we have secured a job promotion by less-than-honest means, we will discover sooner or later that the waters are as "bitter as poison." That's because the bitterness that inevitably follows is the result of what G. K. Chesterton said was the only part of Christian theology that absolutely cannot be denied: sin.[2] Whenever you and I make a decision that involves breaking the law of God, whenever we choose something other than "the holy and right and good" will of God (Romans 7:12, NLT), we are engaging in something named by that three letter word *sin*. Simply put, sin is everything that is out of harmony with God's will for us. You see, God designed all of us to live holy lives; that's why, when our lives are out of harmony with that design, pain and bitterness are sure to follow.

I'll be the first to admit that I don't know much about cars. But I do know that if a person puts diesel fuel into an engine that was designed to run on gasoline, trouble will follow. The car may run for a while, but not smoothly; the driver's future will probably include a lot of smoke; and eventually the engine will shut down until all the diesel fuel is siphoned out and replaced with gasoline. God's original design was that humankind would live by His law. We were designed to perform optimally when we conformed ourselves to His will. But somewhere along the line, someone thought it would be a good idea to fill our tanks with a little "diesel fuel," and the results have been devastating.

In the beginning

Our first parents learned the hard way what happens when people ignore God's will. Back in the very beginning, God placed Adam and Eve in the Garden of Eden and gave them plenty of options for their sustenance. He told the happy couple, "You may freely eat the fruit of every tree in the garden" (Genesis 2:16, NLT). Now, I don't know exactly how many trees there were in that Garden; any number I came up with would be pure conjecture. But I'm quite sure God made more than two or three trees available to them. Perhaps there were a thousand trees, or five million trees, or maybe it was just ten. However many it was, we can be sure that God, being the loving God that He is, gave them a full menu of options. The sky was the limit.

Yet, God tacked a little addendum onto His instructions—a very, very simple one. While Adam and Eve were free to eat from every tree in the Garden, He told them they were to avoid *one* of those trees. They were not to eat from the "tree of the knowledge of good and evil" because if they ate from it, death would surely follow (verse 17).

Of course, you know what happened. Adam and Eve saw the forbidden fruit, and supposing it to taste sweet, they disobeyed God and indulged their lustful appetite. And soon everything changed. The sky turned dark. A cold wind swept through the Garden. And Adam and Eve recognized that they were naked. The equilibrium of their world had been forever altered.

What God asked of them seems like such a small thing. He didn't talk about murder. He didn't bring up the matter of staying faithful to their marital vows. He simply told them they could eat from *every tree in the Garden except one.* This should tell us that no act of disobedience is minor in God's eyes. That's because, in the end, any act of disobedience, whether "big" or "small," reveals a rebellious heart—a heart that has chosen self over God, death over life.

A few months ago I was speaking to a group of teenagers about relationships, and I was encouraging them to put off dating until they were more mature—certainly, a simple piece of advice. During a question-and-answer time after my talk, a young man raised his hand and asked, "So, are you saying that dating is a sin?" Now, for most people, this would be a "no-brainer." Of course it isn't a sin to date—after all, which of the Ten Commandments is a teenager breaking by entering into a relationship prematurely? So perhaps most people would consider my answer to be crazy. I told the teenager "Yes and No." Then I went on to say, "Any time God invites us to do something and we don't do it, or any time He invites us *not* to do something, and we do it, we are sinning."

Adam and Eve's story should tell us as much. The request God made of them seems very inconsequential. They probably thought that eating from the tree really wasn't that big a deal. They weren't, after all, breaking the letter of one of God's ten commandments. Neither of those tables of stone says, "Thou shalt not eat of the tree of the knowledge of good and evil." Yet their decision, however unimportant we might consider it to be, was an act of rebellion—a decision to go their own way instead of God's. And that's what sin is all about.

The prophet Isaiah tells us that "all we like sheep have gone astray; we have turned, every one, to his own way" (Isaiah 53:6). God has placed a road map in front of us. No, better yet, God comes down to each and every one of us and serves as a personal GPS unit on the dashboard of our car. I don't know whether or not He speaks to us with a British accent, but by means of His law He tells us the right way to go. Unfortunately, however, we all—every single one of us—have decided to go our own way. We have been tricked into thinking that another road offers more adventure, is more fulfilling.

All the while we're following a different course than the one He's prescribed, there's a voice patiently saying to us at every wrong turn, "Please turn around. Please turn around." But all of us ignore those instructions at one time or another. We drive faster and faster down the wrong road until we find ourselves lost in the middle of nowhere. All this sin wreaks havoc in our lives, and, if we continue down the wrong road, eventually we'll no longer be able to hear the voice that's saying "Please turn around." It's not that God will have tired of trying to help us get on the right road. It's just that our batteries will have died.

The stroke of a butterfly's wing

Some scientists postulate that the flap of an insect's wing could start a series of events that eventuates in a hurricane or tornado halfway around the world. The theory is called the butterfly effect, and the underlying idea is that seemingly small actions can have far-reaching effects. Those who subscribe to global warming or climate change or whatever one chooses to call it, buy into a similar concept. They propose that human beings, as finite as we are, have a huge part to play in the stability of our climate and natural environment. The point is that we should never underestimate the impact of one decision, however miniscule it might seem to us.

Whether or not one buys into these theories doesn't change the reality that poet John Donne understood long ago. "No man is an island, entire of itself," he penned. "Any man's death diminishes me, because I am involved in mankind; and therefore never send to know for whom the bell tolls; it tolls for thee."[3]

Simply put, we don't live in isolation—we can't even if we try to. What I do affects my neighbor and my neighbor's neighbor and even *your* neighbor. Thus, as Donne declared, one person's death affects everyone else. One person's choice does too. I mention this because it has a lot to do with the topic of the last chapter. There, I discussed the idea that God has created us with incredible freedom, but that freedom holds also the potential of pain. So, if we lay the blame for all the problems of this world at God's doorstep, we misunderstand. Think about this: if God allows us to make our own choices and follow our own paths, and the human race—and the individuals that comprise that human race—have made one bad choice after another, where do you think we should be right now? In truth, it's amazing we haven't already destroyed ourselves. (More on that later.) The point is that the hurtful things we see in the world right now—natural disasters, wars, famines, divorce, pedophilia, genocide—are all the result of years and years and years (*millennia,* actually) of bad decisions; of sin piling upon sin.

Needless to say, Adam and Eve's wrong turn in the very beginning has had an enormous butterfly effect. Because of their sin, all of us are prone to making wrong choices. All of us are inclined to sin. In fact, the Bible says that "there is none who seeks after God" (Romans 3:11). So—and this is the ultimate paradox—human beings were created to seek after God, yet because of Adam and Eve's sin, seeking after God and keeping His law no longer comes naturally to us. We don't want to heed His GPS directions and drive down the road He tells us to follow.

The results of our inborn bias against God's directions have been devastating, because the reality is that what we call *sin* is also *selfishness*. We don't have to peruse the pages of a newspaper very long to realize this. The stock market crashes because a bunch of corporate moguls got a little too greedy. A suicide bomber wipes out dozens of people because he dreams of paradise with seventy-two virgins. A young man rapes a girl because he wants control and the thrill of forbidden sex. The world's inhabitants—you and I included—have done selfish act after selfish act after selfish act. That's why God has to pursue us. We've gotten so far off the right road that we simply cannot find our way back to it—nor do any of us, when left to our own devices, even want to go there.

But it isn't some mere intellectual decision God has made that sends Him searching for us. Every time someone sins, God's heart is wrenched with incredible anguish because that wrong choice hurts and ultimately destroys both the person who made that choice and other people, the innocent as well as the guilty. And just as the love of good parents for their children moves them to do all they can to protect their children, so God's love compels Him to try to protect us.

Of course, it takes a great deal of humility for us to admit that we have lost our way and need someone to find us—to admit that we need to be pursued by God. Since selfishness is the basic force of our nature, only a supernatural act can compel us to recognize, admit, and turn away from our sinfulness. But that can happen. This universe is run by Someone who specializes in supernatural acts.

Back in the early twentieth century, *The Times* of London invited a number of notable authors to write essays on the topic What's Wrong With the World? One distinguished gentleman wrote his essay in the form of a letter. It read, simply, "Dears sirs, I am. Sincerely yours, G. K. Chesterton."[4]

The middle letter of the word *sin* is "I." We need only look in a mirror to see the enemy. Left to our own devices, we wreak incredible havoc that extends to the farthest reaches of the earth—no, the universe. And so God pursues.

CHAPTER SIX

RECONCILIATION

Imagine that you are observing Adam and Eve in the Garden of Eden. They've just eaten the forbidden fruit, and suddenly their whole world has been turned upside down. What emotions do you think ran through their inner being when they realized what they'd done? Confusion? Fear? Terror? Anxiety? Disappointment? Emptiness?

They probably experienced all these emotions and more. I'm sure they also felt deceived; after all, the serpent promised them the world—and more—if they simply ate the fruit. "Your eyes will be opened," he said, "and you will be like God" (Genesis 3:5). That isn't what they experienced, however. In fact, they experienced just the opposite. They'd been created in "the image of God," but now that image had been incredibly marred, and instead of directing them toward God, their nature inclined them to run away from Him.

Genesis tells us as much. Soon after Adam and Eve had eaten the fruit from the tree, they heard God's voice as He was walking in the Garden—and they hid from Him. This little vignette of their experience after their fall into sin provides what may be the most profound insight into the whole human predicament and into God's intention to solve it. It's really a microcosm of the rest of the Bible. Quite frankly, this one verse alone would probably be all we need to understand the gospel. Perhaps I'm overstating the case a little bit, but read the verse for yourself: "They heard the voice of the LORD God walking in the garden in the cool of the day, and Adam and his wife hid themselves from the presence of the LORD God among the trees of the garden" (Genesis 3:8).

Think about this: Adam and Eve—who up to that time had enjoyed complete at-one-ment with God—have just violated God's law. He had told them not to eat of the tree of the knowledge of good and evil, but they had done just that. Prior to this they had never known what it was like to be at odds with God. They had never known what it was like to be on a different page than He was on. They had never been out of harmony with Him. Now they know, and their first reaction is *Uh-oh!*

I don't know about you, but when I wrong someone, when I sin against someone, I immediately feel uncomfortable and apprehensive when I'm near that person. Sensitivities are heightened. Anxiety rises. I interpret any distance between myself and that person as an indication that he is upset with me or disapproves of my behavior. I think he may not care for me anymore. I feel guilty, and often I want to avoid that person altogether.

I'm sure you know from experience how, when you've wronged someone and then see that person at the grocery store or at church or somewhere else, you purposely change your route so you don't have to make eye contact. No doubt you've experienced the reverse as well: you notice that the person who borrowed your electric drill and never gave it back and the one who slandered your name to your co-workers don't seem to show their face to you anymore. And if they do, your conversations are very short and they revolve around very general things—the weather or the economy—and frequently there are moments of incredibly awkward silence. This is what sin does. Fallen human nature tempts us to run away from the person we've wronged instead of toward that person.

And if we react that way toward people we've wronged, how

much more so when we've wronged God. If sin is taking a different path than the one God calls us to, what follows in the wake of sin is the attempt to separate ourselves even further from Him. This is exactly what Adam and Eve did—they tried to hide themselves from God.

He wanted reconciliation

Of course, God knew all this; that's precisely why He did what He did. He knows that sinful people will analyze the behavior of the person they've wronged and interpret any distance as a sure sign of that person's displeasure, so He didn't let Adam and Eve get away from Him. He pursued reconciliation with them. He was quick to remove all doubt they had about Him.

As I've noted above, in spite of God's pursuit of reconciliation—or perhaps because of it—Adam and Eve felt guilt well up inside of their hearts, and they ran the other way. They did so because God's holiness—His love, His grace, His mercy, His justice—is so contrary to the sinful human psyche that we get confused by it and we even fear it. After all, our human nature pushes us to attack those who have wronged us, and when someone else reacts differently to our wronging them, we feel very uncomfortable.

Many translations of Genesis say that after Adam and Eve sinned, they hid from God's "presence." Actually, something a little more nuanced is going on here. The word translated "presence" here literally means "face." Adam and Eve couldn't bear to see God's face. They'd been able to look at it before, when they were sinless. They looked into it and saw the very essence of God's character and found it attractive. But now they couldn't stand to see God's face.

Quite significantly, this Hebrew word meaning "face" pops up again and again in the Bible. In Exodus 33, Moses implores God to show him His glory. In response, God says that He will show Moses His goodness, but He cannot show him His face—"for," God explains, "no man shall see Me, and live" (Exodus 33:20). Later on, the prophet Isaiah shares a profound insight when he informs us that our sins have separated us from God and have "hidden His face from" us (Isaiah 59:2).

Sin builds a barrier, a wall of separation, between God and us. It's true that this barrier is the result of our own guilt and shame. Because of our sins, our shortcomings, our misdeeds, we feel ashamed to be in God's presence and see His face. We can't hang on to sin and at the same time stand in God's presence and look into His face.

But it's also true that sin—and those holding on to sin—simply cannot be in God's presence without suffering dire consequences. When we sinners feel uncomfortable in God's presence, it's not simply because we have a subjective misunderstanding of God that causes us to *feel* as if He disapproves of sin and of us when we hold on to it—as if the feeling of being at odds with Him is a mistake. If we choose to hold on to sin, we actually *are* at odds with Him—not because God doesn't love us anymore or because He no longer wants to save us, but because sin is so contrary to what He's all about that He can't tolerate it in His presence. He can't be true to Himself and at the same time accommodate sin—its self-centeredness, its self-destructive nature. For God to ignore sin would be akin to a paramedic looking the other way when a woman is choking on her lunch at the table next to him. It's a contradiction of God's very essence.

So let's be clear on this: feeling guilty in the wake of violating God's law is a good thing, not a bad thing. People can't fully appreciate for-giveness if they haven't felt guilty. Guilt is evidence that the Holy Spirit is working upon the heart; it isn't a mere mistaken, subjective perception. Adam and Eve's story would have been much different if they hadn't felt any guilt about what they'd done.

It isn't the total absence of guilt that's the opposite of hopeless despair. Instead, it's the feeling of full forgiveness despite one's guilt. That's why God did what He did. Knowing the Holy Spirit's con-victing power and the tendency of humans to react with fear, He made sure that Adam and Eve understood what was preeminent in His heart. Quite simply, His priority is reconciliation—so He pur-sued the sinners. He didn't wait for them to make the first move. Left to themselves, they would probably have run so fast and so far in their attempt to distance themselves from God that they would have died of exhaustion. But before they were overwhelmed with shame and guilt, God took the first step toward reconciliation—He called out to them.

The voice they feared

No doubt Adam and Eve shuddered when they heard God's voice. Guilty people—or at least those who feel their guilt—generally avoid rule-makers. They don't like to see those flashing blue lights when they're going twenty miles per hour over the speed limit, nor do people who have just gotten out of the bed of someone who's not their spouse like seeing their pastor's phone number come up on their caller ID. They expect to have the book thrown at them. Judgment looms.

But something unexpected happens when God pursues Adam and Eve. Instead of condemning them, He asks them questions—four questions in fact. And when He's heard from them and then speaks, it's to curse the serpent who tempted Adam and Eve. He tells the serpent, "I'm declaring war between you and the Woman, between your offspring and hers" (Genesis 3:15, *The Message*), and He promises Adam and Eve His full support. Yes, they've sinned, but the devil has chosen to pick on the wrong people.

No doubt that was one of the greatest turnarounds in history. Adam and Eve were bracing for the worst. They were running away from what they were convinced was an angry and vengeful God. When they heard His voice and realized they weren't going to be able to get away from Him, they started preparing their arguments. ("She made me do it" was all Adam could come up with.) But even after their defense fell flat, God didn't condemn them. Instead, He was eager to do whatever He could to bring them back into harmony with His love and His law.

The truth is that far too often—maybe always—we humans think of God as bent on condemning us, when in reality He leans instead toward compassion and reconciliation. Yes, God's personal Agent, the Holy Spirit, convicts us of the wrongfulness of our sin, but He's just trying to soften our hearts so that we can experience the enormity of His grace and mercy.

Some of us have been holding on to guilt and shame for years— maybe even decades. We're overwhelmed with the weight of promises broken, lies told, duties neglected—and on and on the list goes. The sadness, disappointment, and guilt we feel aren't bad. It's evidence that the Holy Spirit is working upon our hearts. The condemnation our own heart lays upon us combined with the conviction the Holy Spirit raises within us brings us to the breaking point.

The devil wants to keep us there. He wants us to keep running. He wants to keep us silent when God cries out in the tenderest voice the universe has ever known, "Where are you?"

Another vignette

Interestingly, we see another vignette of this human-God dynamic in the story of the woman who was brought before Jesus while He was teaching in the temple. Someone finds her in bed with a man who isn't her husband. The accusers remind Jesus that according to the law, she should be stoned. "What shall we do?" they ask.

Jesus stoops and starts scribbling in the sand. Then the accusers see Jesus look up, and they hear Him say, "He that is without sin among you, let him cast the first stone." The woman, who is lying on the dirt trembling and naked, raises her hands to her head protectively, bracing for the imminent onslaught. Jesus has just written her death sentence.

Then, surprisingly, she hears footsteps slowly and deliberately retreating from her. She dare not look up, however, so she listens—she just listens—until there are no more footsteps. She looks up and sees Jesus, who has stooped to her level, and she sees that face, the face— veiled though it may be by His humanity—of God.

But then something flashes through her hurting psyche. In all the stories, all the anecdotes that she's heard about this Man, He has never so much as said a coarse word. He has never sinned. He is perfect. And now, she supposes, having rid Himself of all the witnesses, the one Man who is truly without sin is going to seal her condemnation.

His mouth opens and His voice—the same voice that Adam and Eve heard in the Garden of Eden soon after they disobeyed—sounds. She anticipates hearing His words of condemnation, but instead from the depths of His soul comes something unexpected. It isn't her last rites. It isn't a catalogue of her wrongdoing. It isn't a statement at all. It's a question. "Woman," Jesus says to her in the most beautiful voice she has ever heard, "where are your accusers? Has no one condemned you?"

The answer is obvious, of course. Her accusers have left. They've gone—gone to who-knows-where. No one is left to condemn her—except the only One who had any right to do so.

Almost before she can acknowledge that her accusers are no longer around, that no one has condemned her, before she shudders at the thought that Jesus might actually be the One who condemns her, He makes His judgment as clear as the noonday sun: "Neither do I condemn you; go and sin no more."

Burdens lifted.

Guilt expunged.

Anxiety released.

Appreciation born.

In the face of Jesus, that woman saw the heart of God.

Adam and Eve saw His face in the Garden of Eden. Moses and David and Solomon and Isaiah and—you name them—they all saw it. We can too. The heart of the Creator God is full of compassion and grace. He delights in pursuing us.

No, He can't simply pretend we never sinned. But He can forgive us because—as we will see in the following pages—He has resolved the sin problem.

CHAPTER SEVEN

RETROCAUSALITY

I'm going to step out on a limb and guess that you don't believe in time travel. Of course, I may be wrong; I have met a few people who subscribe to the theory—but they seem to have had a few other issues going on in their lives that made me wonder about their sanity.

Believe it or not, there are sane and intelligent scientists who flirt with the idea of time travel. They see in the laws of nature the framework necessary to make it possible. Now, I'm not a scientist or the son of a scientist, but I haven't found the case to be compelling. To subscribe to the idea or even to give it serious consideration, one has to have certain philosophical presuppositions about the way time works, and I can't go there.

Yet there is one branch of this subject that does have me intrigued. Though it isn't synonymous with time travel, it is closely related. The theory is called *retrocausality*. Admittedly, this is a strange word, but it does convey what the theory is all about. *Retro* speaks of the past— you could use it of the clothes your grandfather wears—and *causality* refers to something that causes something else to happen. So, *retrocausality* means causality that works "backward in time."[1] In other words, if your eating something for lunch today caused something to happen to you yesterday, that would be an example of retrocausality.

And so would a case of the present being affected by something that won't happen till next year. Some scientists have conducted thought experiments on this theory and are optimistic that physical experiments will soon prove its truth.

No doubt this theory sounds just as outlandish to you as time travel does. I'm pretty much in your boat on that. But there is something about this idea that gives me pause, and I think you might be open to the implications of it as well. In order for us to see whether retrocausality is true, we need to conduct a few theological thought experiments and probe a little bit beneath the previous chapter's narrative.

"Thou shalt surely die"

Soon after God created Adam and Eve, He told them about the privileges and opportunities they had. But He also forbade them to do one thing. He told them they could eat from every tree in the Garden except one—"for," He warned, *"in the day that thou eatest thereof thou shalt surely die"* (Genesis 2:17, KJV; emphasis added).

As we already discovered, Adam and Eve *did* eat from that tree—but curiously, they didn't die—not that day, not the next day, not the next week, month, or year. In fact, Adam lived to the ripe old age of 930! I've had some long days in my life, as you probably have also, but 930 years has to be the longest "day" ever! This is a bit puzzling, to say the least.

Some have pointed out—and rightfully so—that the way our English versions translate this passage can be a bit misleading. The Hebrew literally says "dying, you shall die." This seems to imply that God wasn't necessarily declaring that they would die the very instant they ate the fruit, but that the dying process would begin then—and just as surely as the dying process began, so it would reach its conclusion in death, which turned out to be 930 years later for Adam.

No doubt this explanation comes close to explaining the delay, *but 930 years later?* It seems there must be more to it—after all, even if God hadn't said "in the day," Adam and Eve *still* should have met their end immediately. Scripture seems to indicate that when we choose to disconnect from God, we are disconnecting from our life's source. "All those who hate me," God declares through wisdom's voice, "love death" (Proverbs 8:36, NKJV). And Paul says that the "wages of sin is death" (Romans 6:23). Thus, whether it's Adam and Eve or you and me, the second we choose our own way rather than God's, we are severing our connection with our life source, which logically means we die. At least, it seems that's the way it should be, but of course that's not what happens. Even though when we sin we are essentially declaring to God, "I'll sustain my own life apart from You," we still receive God's life-giving power and so avoid the grave, at least for a little while.

Why?

"Well," we say, "God is loving and gracious, and He chooses to allow us to live." Yes, that's true. But remember: while God is gracious, loving, and forgiving, He is also just and has to maintain some kind of order in this universe. If He were to throw out all laws and justice in the name of being loving and gracious, anarchy would surely follow. God's whole universe is founded upon law and order. There's a place for forgiveness and mercy, of course, but within reason—a very good reason that I think will impress your heart with a deeper gratitude and love for this pursuing God.

Foundations

An interesting phrase pops up a handful of times in the New Testament. In fact, it surfaces ten times in the twenty-seven books that comprise this portion of the Bible. The phrase is "the foundation of the world." It's a very interesting phrase because there is more to it than meets the eye. The word translated "foundation" literally means "beginning" or "creation," and the word translated "world" is the Greek word *cosmos*.

You've probably come across *cosmos* before. The words *cosmonaut* and *cosmology* are its descendants, and so is the word *cosmetic,* though it's derived from a different nuance of the Greek original. Simply put, the word *cosmos* means not only the world, but also all of God's creative order. Thus, a cosmonaut is someone who travels through space and explores the universe, and a cosmologist is a person who studies the entire universe. So when the biblical authors use the term "the foundation of the world," they are referring to the very beginning, the very genesis, of all that God created—indeed, the very beginning of the entire universe.

I find it intriguing that whenever this phrase appears, it's preceded by only one of two words. Either the authors speak about what happened "before" the creation of the universe or they speak of what has happened "from" or "since" the creation of the universe. It's very enlightening to discover that the biblical authors were interested in what happened "before" and "since" the universe came into existence. In the rest of this chapter we'll look at three usages of this phrase, and in the next chapter we'll consider one more usage.

What Scripture says about what happened "before" the creation of the universe is overwhelming. To begin with, in his epistle to the Ephesians, the apostle Paul beautifully declares that God "chose" us in Christ "before the foundation of the world, that we should be holy and without blame before Him in love" (Ephesians 1:4). What Paul says here seems almost beyond comprehension. It should eliminate any anxiety that any of us might have about our standing with God. Apparently, even before we existed, and, for that matter, before anything else existed, not only did God have us firmly implanted in His mind, but He actually chose us to be His children. This is why the prophet Jeremiah could say that God has loved us with "an everlasting love" (Jeremiah 31:3). Even though we, as temporal and material beings, live inside time, God's love for us is "everlasting"; it existed even before time began. How, then, can we ever doubt His love, His care, His purposes and plans for our lives?

Of course, often we doubt these things precisely because of what we're talking about here. Adam and Eve messed up, and every human being since has followed suit. Our conscience rightfully convicts us of our guilt, and we—not so rightfully—start to doubt God's love for us. But here is the interesting bit: our fall from grace didn't catch God off guard. When Adam and Eve bit into that forbidden fruit, God didn't have to scramble to come up with a plan.

That God knew we would sin and was prepared to save us from the consequences is the very point of the next passage in which the word *before* precedes the phrase that means the creation of the universe. First, Peter reminds his audience that they were not "redeemed with corruptible things . . . but with the precious blood of Christ, as of a lamb without blemish and without spot" (1 Peter 1:18, 19). Then he goes on to write something very fascinating. Continuing to speak of Christ, he declares that "he indeed was foreordained before the foundation of the world, but was manifest in these last times for you" (verse 20). Or, as another version puts it a little more poignantly, "God chose him as your ransom long before the world began, but he has now revealed him to you in these last days" (NLT).

In other words, not only did God choose us to be the recipients of His love and grace *before* time and the universe existed, but He even had already developed the plan that included Christ giving His life on our behalf when His created beings would fall and choose their own way. These plans were made during what the prophet Zechariah called the "counsel of peace" (Zechariah 6:13). Thus, our salvation, our well-being, our future were far from being afterthoughts in the mind of God. They were at the forefront of His thinking. Even before we existed, God's plan was to pursue us; He had begun that pursuit "before the foundation of the world."

Back to the future

While our heads may allow our hearts to flirt with the idea that God has always loved us and that even before we existed He chose to have a relationship with us, the question about why Adam and Eve didn't drop dead the second they ate from that tree still confronts us. Here's where our final text comes into play—this time, one in which the phrase is preceded by the word *from* rather than the word *before*. John the revelator shares a startlingly heart-gripping idea in this book of his that many people find frightening. In unmistakable terms, he refers to Christ as the "Lamb slain from the foundation of the world" (Revelation 13:8).

Did you catch that? We may look at Christ's crucifixion as happening in A.D. 31, but according to John, Christ has been the Lamb slain from—or, in other words, ever since—the creation of the universe. No, He wasn't the Lamb slain before the universe existed, even though God's plan was in place before His act of creating. But Christ, the Lamb, was slain the *moment* this universe came into being. We might say that even before there was sin, there was a sacrifice. Even before Adam and Eve bit into that fruit, Christ was their Savior.

The implications of this are astounding. Its influence is never ceasing. But how is it possible?

Easy: retrocausality.

We've now come full circle and find ourselves considering the implications of that term. Actually, it's quite simple: when Christ went to the cross four thousand years after Adam and Eve sinned, the effects of His sacrifice shot all the way back in time to the very beginning of the universe. By meeting the demands of justice at Calvary, His death granted life to every created being who would ever rebel against God and try to break away from Him.

Of course, the Bible tells us that Adam and Eve weren't the ones who introduced rebellion into the universe. That happened in heaven some time before they were created, when the "anointed cherub" (see Ezekiel 28:14), Lucifer, turned his back on God and convinced a whole host of angels to do the same. Actually, justice called for him to be blotted out of existence the minute he rebelled against God— rebellion is incompatible with God's presence. So we must reach an astounding, scandalous conclusion: the Cross justified even Lucifer's continued existence! It was only by God's grace that he was allowed to continue living. Unfortunately, even though Lucifer evidently saw a full picture of God's love and grace and may even have glimpsed the Crucifixion before it happened, he sealed his decision by rejecting God's pursuing love for him once and for all. Still more unfortunate, millions of others have followed in his tracks, making the same decision.

The amazing reality is that whether or not we realize it, all of us have been sustained by the cross of Christ. Whether we're thinking of Adam and Eve in the very beginning, or the patriarchs and prophets after them; the scribes, Pharisees, and disciples in Jesus' day, or the pastors, prostitutes, and atheists in our day; all of us have been saved—yes, *saved,* at least temporarily—by the cross of Christ. If it weren't for that cross, none of us would have been given a second chance, or even a second breath, after committing sin. As one thoughtful writer has put it,

> To the death of Christ we owe even this earthly life. The bread we eat is the purchase of His broken body. The water we drink is bought by His spilled blood. Never one, saint or sinner, eats his daily food, but he is nourished by the body and the blood of Christ. The cross of Calvary is stamped on every loaf. It is reflected in every water spring.[2]

The diagram below shows this wonderful truth and just how far-reaching the effect of the Cross is.

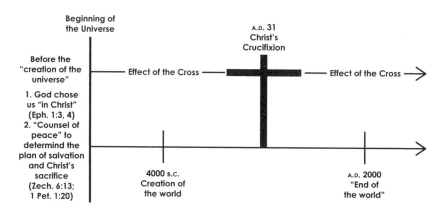

So, those who lived before Christ's incarnation—even before this world was brought into existence—were upheld by the Cross. This may seem like an astonishing idea, but if we recognize that Christ was the Lamb slain from the beginning of the universe, this must be the case. If justice demands the application of its penalties on those who sin against God, then sinners—including even Lucifer—can continue living only because someone sustained their lives by taking their punishment. Similarly, all those who have lived on this side of Christ's crucifixion have also been upheld by that Cross, and this effect of the Cross will continue on into eternity, since the redeemed can live forever only because Jesus satisfied justice on Calvary. So, the effect of the Cross reaches back to the very beginning of time itself, and it reaches forward into the ceaseless ages of eternity. This, to me, is mind-boggling. There, on Calvary's tree, we see the most profound mystery of all mysteries. God in His great mercy decided that all of us were valuable enough to be worth saving from destruction. And the sacrifice He made—an infinite sacrifice—has touched *every single created being in the universe* whether or not they realize it.

Jesus alluded to the universal implications of His death when He proclaimed, "I, if I be lifted up from the earth, will draw all men unto me" (John 12:32, KJV). Truth be told, the original Greek of this passage doesn't have the word *men;* the translators added that word. Jesus just said, "I . . . will draw all unto me." I read this as meaning that through His death, He has drawn *all* of His created order—in other words, the entire universe—to Himself. He has met the demands of justice for even the most hard-hearted sinner; and eventually, every created being—even Satan, himself—will bow to Christ and proclaim His Lordship and His love (see Philippians 2:10, 11; Revelation 15:3, 4)—all this because of the Cross.

But here's the real clincher for me, one that knocks down any anxiety or doubt the tempter might raise about God's thoughts and feelings toward me. Without any decision on my part—indeed, even before time began—God unilaterally decided to choose me to be His child. And then He unilaterally decided that if I sinned, He would meet the demands of justice for me. And then He unilaterally sent His Son to die for me so that even when I spit in His face and turn my back on Him and tell Him I want to live my life alone, without Him, He *still* sustains me.

All this shows that He's been exercising His grace since the beginning of time—no, even before time began. He's been pursuing me, hoping beyond hope that I will respond to Him. He hopes you'll let Him into your life too. The only question left is whether you and I—sinners that we are—will allow the effect of the Cross to work in our lives throughout eternity.

Our heavenly Pursuer hopes as much.

CHAPTER EIGHT

LOST

OK, I'll admit it: Camille is the only woman I was ever able to persuade to have a romantic relationship with me. I don't know how many attempts I made with various young women, but my track record was anything but stellar.

It wasn't for lack of trying. All through high school and much of college, I was what you would call a "hopeless romantic"—I longed for a relationship with someone of the opposite gender, and certainly tried my hardest to start one, but it was all for naught. Time and time again it seemed that I'd hardly get through the "would you like to . . ." part of the invitation before a worried look would cross the face of the young woman I had approached and she would say something like, "Shawn, you're a really nice guy, but . . ." I can write this now in good humor because, since then, God has given me the best woman in the world!

As I've reflected upon the sad state of affairs I experienced in those days, I've also realized that God was trying to help me understand two things: He was trying to help me understand both my need for Him and His need for me.

To begin with, for far too long I tried to find my fulfillment in romance. Maybe I'm the only man in the world who has experienced this, but often my general attitude toward life was determined by how things were going with the young woman I wanted to date. If things were going well and seeming to be heading toward romance, then I was happy. If not, oh boy, watch out!

You may find it very surprising that I'm admitting to a total lack of success in the romance department, but I believe this was the Lord's way of mercifully helping me see that I wasn't depending on Him, that I wasn't looking to Him as the true source of fulfillment. I needed to redirect my energies, to turn them toward responding to the right Person.

The other part of my insight is important too. I believe God was helping me sense His need of me. I believe that, like me, He has faced rejection time and time again, and, like me, He longs for a relationship of love with each of His sons and daughters.

The relational God

I realize that the idea we're going to look at in this chapter can very easily creep into the clichéd or slide into the sappy. It seems that these days I can hardly pick up a religious book or listen to a sermon without getting the sense that God is a rose-buying, love-song-writing, poetry-reciting chap. Quite frankly, when I encounter such a picture of God, I'm left feeling as though I've just eaten a gallon of ice cream. I'm going to try to avoid doing that to you.

However, I also realize that many of us have never seen God as Someone who loves us passionately. Some come from a religious background that simply has no room for such an idea. Others of us have been given the exact opposite picture of God—that He doesn't care for us unless we conform blindly to His law or even that He's actively out to get us. Most of us find it amazing that the picture of God in both the Old and the New Testaments does in fact border on the sappy, because the reality is that the God of Christianity (and of Judaism) is a God of relationships. In fact, more often than not, the biblical authors couch their explanations of God in the language of relationship. It's because God longs for intimate relationship with others that He gave us life in the beginning and pursues us now. He has always longed for our attention and our love. He longed for it before time began. He has always been, and ever will be, about relationship. Simply put, He is a relational Being; we might even say He is an omni-relational Being: that is, all-relational.[1]

In the previous chapter we looked at two of the three instances in which the Bible gives us insight into what happened "before the foundation of the world." Now we're going to look at the third and final passage that uses this phrase: John 17:24. This verse is part of a prayer that Jesus directs toward His Father. Notice what He says: "Father, I desire that they also whom You gave Me may be with Me where I am, that they may behold My glory which You have given Me; for You loved Me before the foundation of the world."

Notice what Jesus says was happening "before the foundation of the world"—before the universe was created: He declares that His Father "loved" Him! Some may think this idea is obvious, and others may not see its relevance, but I believe this statement gives us incredible insight into the relational nature of God. Before this universe existed, before time began, before there was anyone or anything else, God the Father and God the Son had a mutually loving, mutually caring relationship. Each put the interests and desires of the other above His own. Of course, the Third Member of the Godhead—the Holy Spirit—would also have been involved in this blissful relationship, which was what Skip MacCarty calls a "veritable circle of beneficence."[2]

Proverbs gives us additional insight into this bond, picturing the pre-incarnate Christ saying through the voice of Wisdom, "The LORD possessed me at the beginning of His way, before His works of old. I have been established from everlasting, from the beginning, before there was ever an earth" (Proverbs 8:22, 23). He then goes on to add, "I was beside Him as a master craftsman; and I was daily His delight, rejoicing always before Him" (verse 30). Thus, God the Father, Jesus, and the Spirit not only loved One Another, but They also delighted and rejoiced in Each Other's company.

I don't know about you, but I would have loved to be a fly on the wall when only the Three of Them were all that existed. To be able to witness the fullest and most undivided expressions of love in the universe would have brought even a mere observer unimaginable joy. Perhaps the divine pursuing grace originated among the Godhead in eternity past as each Member of the Trinity unreservedly threw Himself into relationship with the Others.

This divine relationship had an inevitable result: Creation. After all, it's the nature of love and relationship to create—if you don't believe me, just come to my house and see who sleeps in the room across the hall from Camille and me. By definition, love is meant to be shared, and shared with increasingly more "others." (This is why Camille and I would like to have at least eighteen children—though she doesn't realize this yet!) This "veritable circle of beneficence" created the universe—and love spread from Three to three gazillion in about eight seconds flat!

Of course, you know what happened soon after. The relationship was broken. God's creatures, whom He loved with all His heart, turned their backs on Him, saying "No, thank You" to His invitation to relationship, and God found Himself in a bind.

Sanctuary

Before Adam and Eve sinned, God was able to enjoy regular fellowship with them. Because there was nothing in their lives that was out of harmony with Him, they could stand in His presence without shame and without any negative consequences. But all that changed when they ate the forbidden fruit—they fled from Him and tried to hide. Of course, they had reason to—standing before Him while holding on to sin would have ended their lives. That this separation was necessary broke the heart of the relational God. He longed for complete and true fellowship with the people He had made. But they rejected Him—and all of us humans have done the same ever since.

When Moses and the children of Israel left Egypt, God instructed them to build a structure in the midst of their camp: "Let them make

Me a sanctuary," He instructed Moses (Exodus 25:8). Why did God want His people to build Him a sanctuary? He didn't tell them to build a sanctuary in the midst of their camp so He could dazzle them with His majesty and glory. He didn't tell them to build a sanctuary there so they could bring their sacrifices to Him. He didn't even tell them to build a sanctuary so they could understand the rescue plan. No doubt the sanctuary and its services accomplished all these things, but God didn't mention these ends as His reason for having the children of Israel build Him a sanctuary. Instead, He said He wanted His people to build Him a sanctuary so He could "dwell among them"; so He could dwell "in their midst" (*YLT*); so He could "live among them" (*The Message*). Being the "omni-relational" God that He is, He couldn't stand being apart from His creatures. It broke His heart to have so much distance between Him and them. Thus, He couldn't help Himself. He's like my cousin, who insists on sitting along one side of a table rather than at one of the ends so he can be at the center of all the action. In a way, God feels lost if He isn't right in the middle of blissful communion with us.

Of course, the ultimate revelation of God's relational nature is the incarnation of Christ. We long to go deeper and deeper in our human relationships—and we're not content to stay at arm's length from those we love. That's true of God too. Though the sanctuary enabled Him to dwell among His sinful people, it didn't provide a complete relationship. Moses was the only one who enjoyed face-to-face communion with God; the rest of His people were too afraid to come close to Him, completely misunderstanding why God set up His home in the middle of their camp. Though He really meant the sanctuary for relationship, they thought it was all about sacrifice and appeasement. So God stepped it up a notch. Jesus entered into the world as an actual human being with a literal human body and a real human nature.

Couching the Incarnation in terminology that would turn a light on in the minds of those with a background in Israel's history, John boldly proclaimed in his Gospel that "the Word became flesh and dwelt among us" (John 1:14, NKJV). The word translated "dwelt" literally means "tabernacle." It harkened back to what God had been trying to accomplish all along: renewing His relationship with people. He wasn't content with living in a house in the middle of the neighborhood where no one visited. Motivated by His pursuing love, God decided to open the front door wide. If His people wouldn't come to Him, He would chase after them—which is what He'd been up to all along anyway.

Jesus spent His whole life on earth pursuing the lost. For thirty years He sat at wells, feasted at homes, and preached on hillsides—all in the grand pursuit of relationship. He wasn't content to sit in His heavenly mansion without the fellowship of His creatures. He felt lost without that fellowship—and He still does.

Don't get me wrong: God doesn't need us in the way we need air. But He probably does need us a lot more than we realize—probably the same way Camille and I, though fully enjoying companionship with one another before we became parents, needed a child when we were without one. After my son came into the world, my "need" for him increased tenfold. I believe that in the same way, now that we creatures have arrived on God's radar screen, His need for us has multiplied exponentially.

How do I know?

Because I'm a father.

Father knows best

Not long after Camille and I welcomed Camden into the world, we had to cart him to Maine for some meetings. My responsibilities included helping with meetings aimed at teenagers. Unfortunately, Camille was roped into teaching sign language to kids nine to twelve years old at the same time that I had to be carrying out my assignments. Usually, that meant she would bring him to the church where our youth meetings were being held, hand him to me, and then go to her meeting. I would sit in the back of the church holding Camden for about fifteen minutes, when Camille, having completed her brief class, came back to pick him up again.

While I was holding Camden one night, I had an "aha!" moment. Camden was resting on my lap and looking up at my face, and the group in the church was singing a song that I'd heard a million times before and didn't much care for—mostly because its lyrics are repetitive. But for an instant that evening everything came together. As I stared into Camden's eyes, I heard the group sing four simple words that long ago had become rote and meaningless to me. This time, however, they slammed into me like a typhoon.

The four words were: *I'm. Lost. Without. You.* They sound like such a cliché, something that three years ago would have caused me to roll my eyes. But now I know them to be undeniably true. The reality is that I can't imagine my life without Camden—and suddenly I realized *that's how God feels about us!*

Unbelievable as it sounds, God feels lost without us. That's why He labored and pleaded so long with His people Israel. That's what moved Him to ask, using imagery that makes a whole lot more sense to me now, "Can a woman forget her nursing child, and not have compassion on the son of her womb? Surely they may forget, yet I will not forget you. See, I have inscribed you on the palms of My hands" (Isaiah 49:15, 16). It's what caused the prodigal father in Luke 15 to spend every evening scanning the horizon—hoping, praying, wondering if his lost son would return home. And, of course, it is what caused God to send His Son Jesus to die in place of His other sons and daughters. He's done all this because He feels lost without us. This reveals the heart of the omni-relational—and, might I add, omni-pursuing—God that the Bible uplifts. He yearns to have a relationship with us. He can't stand to be apart from us.

Sappy though it may sound, does it not tug at your heartstrings? It's hard to believe the lengths to which this omni-relational God has gone—and continues to go—to open our eyes to the reality of His pursuing love and grace. He tries and tries and tries again to help us see that all He has ever wanted from us was the slightest indication that we, too, want a relationship with Him; that we no longer want to take our own path, to go our own way—a way that leads us far from an all-encompassing relationship with Him.

CHAPTER NINE

A DAY FOR US

Let me set the scene for you: I am in Wal-Mart with Camille and Camden. It's my day off. Camden is strapped into the cart, and I'm pushing. He "oohs" and "aahs" at various items in the store as Camille leads the charge.

Suddenly, I feel something buzz in my pocket. Realizing that it's my cell phone, I reach into my pocket, retrieve it, flip it open, and see that I have a text message. It's from a church member, and now I'm faced with a dilemma: to read it or not to read it. It *is* my day off, after all. But, predictably, I can't resist. Spending three seconds reading a 160-character-long message seems harmless, so I go ahead and scroll through it. Of course, now I'm faced with another dilemma: Do I or do I not respond? Responding will take all of twenty seconds, and besides, Camille is rummaging through racks of baby clothes and commenting about diaper deals. These aren't exactly subjects that I daydream about, so I put my thumb to the keypad and start typing away. And then, almost as if she has a sixth sense, Camille looks up from the rack, sees what I'm doing, and says, "Shawn, will you stop texting! Can't we have a day just for *us*?"

Ouch!

Now, don't start acting smug. Come on, admit it—you've been

there too! You've texted at the dinner table, pored over e-mails while on vacation, and surfed the Web while you stood in the checkout line at the grocery store—all the while ignoring the real people who really are in your vicinity, who have real information and real stories to share with you.

In a word, we are ignoring relationships.

I don't suppose I'm sharing anything earth-shattering here, but the truth is that as the world becomes more connected, we're becoming more and more disconnected from one another. And, interestingly, the scientific world is discovering that all this so-called multitasking—which modern technology makes easy to attempt—is taking its toll on our lives and our brains. While technology companies continue to produce more gadgets and more games to fill the gaps in our day and entertain us during our "micro-moments," our brains suffer. Ironically, we're also more bored than ever before.

"People think they're refreshing themselves," says Marc Berman, a neuroscientist at the University of Michigan, "but they're fatiguing themselves."[1] One groundbreaking study from the University of Michigan, for example, showed that when people take a walk in nature, they were "significantly better" at learning than when they went for a walk in the city, "suggesting that processing a barrage of information leaves people fatigued."[2] The constant distractions with which we fill our lives are actually re-wiring our brains and making it harder for us to focus, filter out irrelevant information, and retain what we've learned. Our short-term memory capacity is dwindling, and our stress levels are at an all-time high.

But we don't get it. And the problem is troubling children at younger and younger ages. When author Richard Louv traveled across America, asking school children about their recreational habits, fourth-grader Paul responded with all the sincerity his heart could muster. "I like to play indoors better," he said, " 'cause that's where all the electrical outlets are."[3]

Perhaps what is most troubling, however, is not what's happening to our cognitive abilities, but what's happening to our relational pursuits. This is why Stanford University communications professor Richard Nass worries that our spending so much time using technology is taking a toll on our ability to empathize, since we are "limiting how much we engage with one another, even [with those] in the same room."[4]

Simply put, many people the world over long for what Camille longed for that day—and still longs for from time to time: "Can't we have a day just for *us*?"

A day for us

As I have reflected on this phenomenon of distraction, my mind turns somewhere else. There's no doubt that as our lives get busier and busier and we fill our days with more and more activity, our human relationships suffer greatly. I've sat in rooms for hours at a time during which the only interaction between the people there involved one person showing the others a picture from a friend's Facebook page.

Short-changing our human relationships is a tragedy to be sure, but Someone else has suffered far more than our family and friends. You remember that omni-relational Fellow we talked about in the last chapter? He is the silent Guest in that room, hardly noticed as we surf the Internet and flip through the television channels. Don't get me wrong: it isn't just the increase in technological products that has distracted us from Him. The history of humankind shows us that distractions have abounded in every age—though I would still contend that it is a whole lot easier to ignore this silent Guest now, when multiple screens vie with each other for our attention. So, like Camille, this omni-relational, silent Guest asks, "Can't we have a day that is just for *us*?"

In fact, there *is* a day that is just for "us," and it's been around for millennia. So relationally oriented and so other-centered is God that He has set aside a whole day every week to be kept free from all distractions and devoted entirely to relationship building. Scripture tells us that in the very beginning, in Eden's perfect state, after God finished all His creative work, He "rested on the seventh day" and "blessed . . . and sanctified it" (Genesis 2:2, 3).

This one little thought is so power-packed that we need to make sure we don't miss one ounce of its good news. After spending six days creating this world, God didn't simply sign off. Instead, He spent a day—a whole twenty-four-hour period—enjoying what He had just created. A part of that creation, of course, was humankind. In fact, it was just the day before, on the sixth day of the week, that God formed Adam and Eve. But notice: after He created them, He didn't say to them, "Hey, can you wait here while I go and make some more stuff?" Instead, the very next day, He cleared His schedule, so to speak, and spent a whole day with them. The three of them enjoyed His creation together.

This, to me, is the ultimate picture of an omni-relational God. He orchestrated the Creation week in such a way that Adam and Eve spent the first full day of their existence in His presence, free from all other distractions. Neither He nor they had any other obligations. He could very easily have created Adam and Eve and said to them, "All right, get to work. You get to spend the rest of your lives in useful labor while enjoying My presence in 'micro-moments' scattered through your busy days." But He didn't do that. Instead, He created *a whole day* that had no other purpose than to foster relationship. Every other day of the Creation week was filled with the work of creating light, plants, animals, or the other things He brought into existence. But He didn't create anything on the seventh day of the Creation week. That day was meant for nothing other than fellowship. We might even say it was a day to create relationship. This is probably why God valued the day so much and "sanctified it," which simply means that He made it "holy." The seventh day of the week is the first thing the Bible says God made holy. He saw the tremendous benefit the day could bring by reserving time when both He and His creation could unplug from the distractions and plug into each other.

What does the Bible mean when it says something is "holy"? The next time the word appears in the Hebrew Bible, it's in a story that can help us understand it. When Moses has fled from Egypt and is tending sheep in the desert, he happens upon a very intriguing scene. There before him on one of the slopes of Mount Horeb, a bush is on fire but isn't burning up. Curious, he ventures closer—until he hears an unmistakable voice. It's God's voice, and He tells Moses, "Take your sandals off your feet, for the place where you stand is holy ground" (Exodus 3:5).

There was nothing inherently better about this particular spot on earth than any other. It was just a normal plot of land that, were you to visit it today, wouldn't look special. One thing made it holy at that particular moment: God's presence. This has been and continues to be the only way for anything to become holy. Thus, when Scripture says God made the seventh day holy, it means that He graced it— and continues to grace it—with His presence. Although God is, of course, present on the other six days of the week, just as He was present over all the earth when He declared to Moses that the land around the burning bush was "holy," something far grander fills the seventh day of the week. In that day, also known as the "Sabbath," we get the fullness of God's presence, His complete attention and focus. And perhaps just as significantly for God, He gets *our* complete presence and attention as well—at least that's what we *should* give Him!

Not surprisingly, when Jesus came to this earth in human flesh, He didn't spend His time tearing down this relationship-enhancing day. Instead, He strengthened it. "The Sabbath was made for man, not man for the Sabbath," He announced to a shocked audience that lived in slavish submission to the seventh day (Mark 2:27). In stating this, Jesus was reiterating what has been God's intent for the day all along. The Sabbath is, after all, in the words of Jewish rabbi Abraham Heschel, "the most precious present mankind has received from the treasure house of God."[5] God intended for His people to enjoy the wonderful gift of the Sabbath in all its beauty so that we would call it a "delight" (Isaiah 58:13). He wanted us to be refreshed by what it does for our relationships—with both God and our fellow human beings.

Unfortunately, the Jews in Jesus' day—and many Jews and Christians in our day—forgot that the Sabbath was a precious gift from God, and they instead made it into a day of dos and don'ts, formulating rigid rules that governed just about every scenario a person could encounter. This isn't to say that they didn't sincerely desire to honor God through the Sabbath; they were just a little misled.

Because they misunderstood the Sabbath, Jesus had to correct their thinking a bit. Thus, He deliberately healed a number of individuals on the Sabbath, reminding His audiences that it is "lawful to do good on the Sabbath" (Matthew 12:12). It was also on this wonderful day that He gave what may be His most glorious invitation: "Come to Me, all you who labor and are heavy laden, and I will give you rest. Take My yoke upon you, and learn from Me, for I am gentle and lowly in heart, and you will find rest for your souls. For My yoke is easy and My burden is light" (Matthew 11:28–30). All this was to show what the grand and glorious purpose of the Sabbath was and is: it is a day for healing, rest, and relationship; a day on which to unwind and enter into undistracted and complete intimacy with our Creator-God and with one another.

Heschel put it this way: "In the tempestuous ocean of time and toil there are islands of stillness where man may enter a harbor and reclaim his dignity. This island is the seventh day, the Sabbath, a day of detachment of things, instruments and practical affairs as well as of attachment to the spirit."[6]

I like that. Amid the crashing waves of our stress-filled lives, the Sabbath is an island that gives us respite and relief. It is an unconditional gift from God that all can benefit by if they wish to.

Elsewhere, Heschel called the Sabbath a glorious "palace in time."[7] I like that too—that the Sabbath is a splendid palace which God invites us to enjoy. We need not go to Buckingham Palace or the White House to encounter royalty; we need only to participate in the weekly, grace-filled joy that only the seventh-day Sabbath gives.

I don't know about you, but the invitation to come and enjoy the Sabbath is mighty refreshing to me. I have found over and over again that I crave the liberation that only the Sabbath can bring. To think that God has actually built into the week a day in which I have the right to ditch my preoccupation with work, money, competition, and all sorts of other things that vie for my attention gives me a deeper appreciation for Him. And I have repeatedly found that accepting Christ's invitation to put all those other things aside and enjoy undistracted fellowship with Him doesn't result in my bank account dwindling, my homework piling up, or the world collapsing. No, quite the opposite. In fact, I have found that when I fully respond to God's Sabbath, I can accomplish more in the six other days of the week than I could if I were to simply bog myself down during all seven.

What about you? Have you felt the Holy Spirit making you discontented with the constant distractions of life in today's world? Have you sensed that your life is being held hostage by the iPhone, e-mail, or fifty-hour work weeks?

Or maybe you're troubled by something other than modern technology. Maybe it's something else that seems to constantly call your name, causing you to forget that there's an omni-relational God who is eager to spend a day—a *whole* day—with you.

The palace in time

In *The Search for God at Harvard,* Ari L. Goldman shares a beautiful picture of what the Sabbath gives the weary soul. Goldman was raised an Orthodox Jew—which is the strictest mainstream branch of Judaism—and his attempt to reconcile Judaism with the world in which he lived made his spiritual life a constant rollercoaster ride.

However, the family in which Goldman grew up was probably an even greater cause of stress for him. His family was extremely dysfunctional. His parents were constantly arguing with one another and accusing each other of everything under the sun. Eventually they divorced, which he didn't feel solved anything at all. In fact, more than thirty years later, he was still trying to get over their divorce. He thought he should be allowed to sue them because of the trauma it caused him.

But amidst all of the chaos that went on in his family, one particular moment inevitably brought peace to the family and particularly to his parents. In a sense, it was a literal haven and refuge for him. Notice how he describes the memories he cherishes.

There was another element of that life that I loved. Friday night. It was a time when, by the magic of the Sabbath candles, we were transformed into a happy, picture-book family. The recriminations and bickering would cease and the music would begin. Dov [his younger brother] was just a baby at the time, but Shalom [his older brother] and I would sit at the gleaming white table in our "Shabbat outfits," dark blue pants and white cotton shirts open at the collar. Our hair was still wet from our pre-Sabbath baths, and it was combed neatly across our foreheads. Yarmulkes were bobby-pinned to our heads. My mother waved her hands over the lighted candles and covered her eyes as she stood in a silent moment of meditation. Afterwards, she took us into her arms and kissed us, lingering an extra moment to drink in our freshness. She told us that we looked like the two angels that tradition says accompany the men home from the Friday-night synagogue service.

When, a little while later, my father returned from the synagogue, we lined up in front of him for the Sabbath blessing, the eldest, Shalom, first and then me. "May God make you like Ephraim and Menashe," he said invoking the two grandsons of Jacob who, as Joseph's children, were especially beloved. Bending down to reach us, my father cradled our heads between his strong hands as he recited the blessing. "May He bless you and keep you . . . and give you peace."

My father, who worked hard all week managing and selling real estate, became our rabbi and cantor on Friday night. He took us through the meal singing the joyous melodies of the Hasidim and the resolute songs of the Chalutzim, the

Israeli pioneers who, we were told, were singing the same songs as they worked to turn the desert green. My mother, a confirmed "listener" rather than singer, hummed along with a smile of contentment on her face.[8]

Talk about an island refuge to counteract the storms of life! Amidst all the chaos, fighting, and bickering, this family would enter into a weekly respite and enjoy the peace that only heaven can bring. The beautiful experience still rests firmly in this man's mind today.

The same experience can also be ours. We may be bombarded with busyness and strife. We may be up to our ears in work and distractions. We may feel as if we don't have a second to respond to God or to spend with our families. Precisely because of all this, God gives us a weekly, twenty-four-hour-long "palace in time" that we can enter, knowing that, like Goldman's father, God cradles our heads between His strong hands and declares a blessing of peace upon us.

Mystery of all mysteries—this God who pursues us, pursues us even through a day! And He wants nothing more than to bring us true rest, joy, and happiness.

It is for this reason that He gives us the Sabbath.

CHAPTER TEN

THE BOWING AND BENDING AND BEGGARLY GOD

I was mildly amused at the reaction to something that President Barack Obama did. It seemed to raise the ire of numerous political pundits. Some were moderately uncomfortable, and some others were simply left scratching their heads, but many said they were outraged.

What did the president do? He simply took a bow! In fact, he did so on a number of occasions. One of those was when he met with Japanese Emperor Akihito. After shaking his hand, President Obama leaned over and bowed to him. Photographers were there to catch the curious maneuver, and it was soon the buzz in the American media.

As I said, it wasn't the first or last time the president has bowed in the presence of other dignitaries, none of whom bow to him. But each and every time he has taken this posture, it has ignited a firestorm. In particular, I was intrigued by the passionate reflections from one commentator who felt that Obama's actions were disgraceful. "Heads of state do not engage in bows to one another," this person stated. "To show obeisance to a fellow head of state is a mistake. Bowing implies inferiority, and I don't think that's the right signal to send."[1] In essence, this writer felt that Obama was humiliating himself and showing weakness and inferiority, and he believed that bowing isn't the posture that the most powerful being in the world should take.

I don't want to get political about this issue—it doesn't matter whether it was Barack Obama, George Bush, Richard Nixon, or George Washington who bowed. What intrigues me the most is the sentiment shared by many that those in power shouldn't humiliate themselves and act inferior to anyone. Leaders must be strong. They must puff themselves up and maintain a certain level of pride. Humility is weakness. Hubris is strength.

Such is the sentiment of many people. But could it be that the God of the universe—the most powerful Being in existence—bows before His creatures? Could He, rather than demanding deference from His creatures, actually humble Himself before us?

Delight

The prophet Isaiah gives us beautiful insight into God's thoughts toward us. For a long time, God's people Israel were anything but the epitome of what His grace and love were all about. King after king led them deeper into apostasy and further away from God. Their land was filled with violence; the rich exploited the poor; and parents were even sacrificing their children to various gods. To say that God should have been greatly distraught with their behavior would be an understatement.

Yet God still had hope for His people. In fact, through Isaiah, He promised them a Deliverer. "Behold, the virgin shall conceive and bear a Son," God proclaimed, "and shall call His name Immanuel" (Isaiah 7:14). That wonderful name, *Immanuel,* means "God with us." Isaiah's prophecy pointed to how far this omni-relational God would go in His attempts to save us—He would take on human flesh and live among His people. And not only that, but Isaiah indicated later in his book that Immanuel would be "wounded for our transgressions" and "bruised for our iniquities" (Isaiah 53:5). He would take on the sins of the whole world and die in our place.

What was the purpose of God's constant pursuit of human beings? Notice what Isaiah says:

> "You shall no longer be termed Forsaken, nor shall your land any more be termed Desolate; but you shall be called Hephzibah, and your land Beulah; for the LORD delights in you, and your land shall be married. For as a young man marries a virgin, so shall your sons marry you; and as the bridegroom rejoices over the bride, so shall your God rejoice over you" (Isaiah 62:4, 5).

This has to be one of the most beautiful descriptions in all of Scripture! When our lives appear forsaken and desolate, God cuts in and says, "Not so fast . . ." The grand and glorious purpose of God's constant pursuit is to restore us to humankind's Edenic state—back to what Adam and Eve were before they sinned, when they were constantly and transparently connected to their omni-relational God. God calls this relationship "marriage." We'll return to this idea later, but suffice it to say for now that what God is trying to accomplish in this whole pursuit of grace is complete and full intimacy with us, His creatures, and we with Him.

There's a very simple reason for this. Six words in this wonderful passage make that reason clear: "for the LORD delights in you." That's it, pure and simple. Nothing more; nothing less. The God of the universe, the One who made the sun, moon, and stars, and all the galaxies and planets and solar systems—the One who made it all actually "delights" in the little specks of dust that we are. He takes pleasure in us. He enjoys relationship and companionship with us.

This shouldn't be a surprise, of course, because He is, after all, an omni-relational Being. Thus, it is almost as if He is energized when we respond to Him. Our response to His pursuit actually puts a little hop in His step. It puts a smile on His face, just as a "bridegroom rejoices over the bride."

But there is more to this profound mystery that is quite intriguing.

The Hebrew word used here is *chaphets*. And although this word certainly has the meaning of delighting in someone or something, it also has a secondary meaning that has perplexed scholars. This secondary meaning surfaces in only one place in the whole Hebrew Bible—Job 40:17. There, we read that the behemoth, a giant, and as yet unidentified, creature "moves his tail like a cedar." The word translated "move" is *chaphets,* and scholars aren't quite sure what to make of the image being conveyed. Many agree, however, that what Job describes here is a bending motion of the tail. It's actually translated this way in the *New American Standard Bible*. Thus, the word *chaphets* not only means to "delight," but it also seems to have the connotation of bending down.

When I first made this discovery and pondered its implications, I, too, was a bit perplexed. I realized that just because a single Hebrew word has two different meanings doesn't mean that the two meanings are related to one another. After all, we see this in English; when we use the word *right,* we may be referring to a direction or to a privilege—two meanings not necessarily related to each other.

But then something interesting happened as I was thinking about this concept. As I said before, I have the privilege of watching my son in the mornings while my wife works. Most of the time he wakes up after I do, so I have a little personal time during which I read my Bible and interact with God. On a morning when I was studying this passage in Isaiah, I heard Camden's innocent little voice through the baby monitor. I went upstairs and lifted him out of his crib, and the two of us retreated to the living room to enjoy one another's company.

As I often do, I laid him down on his back and talked to him a bit, and then started to tickle him, which caused his little belly to shake and his laughter to echo through the house. I couldn't help myself then. I simply couldn't. I was finding so much delight in him that I bent down and plopped my big body right there on the floor next to him and started tickling him some more. I loved being with him!

And then it hit me: this was *chaphets* in all its fullness—I was bending low to take pleasure in Camden! Instead of sitting on the couch with my arms folded across my chest, I couldn't help but come down to his level and roll around on the floor with him. And that's when I truly was delighting in him. It was then that I truly lost any sense of self and was caught up in the joy of humble pleasure in him. The center of my life was no longer me, but him.

This is where "delight" and "bending low" are connected. It is precisely because God delights in us that He centers His activities on us. In fact, this omni-relational God takes such delight in us that He bent to the lowest point of the universe's existence on our behalf.

Yes, for us, the God of the universe bows.

How low can you go?

Paul actually shows us a picture of perhaps the lowest bow anyone has ever taken. It is recorded in his letter to the Philippians and is a reflection of the length to which our delighting and bending God went.

In this epistle, Paul challenges his readers to let go of their selfish prerogatives and embrace a particular posture—a counter-intuitive one. He does this by pointing to Christ's example, saying that He,

being in the form of God, did not consider it robbery to be equal with God, but made Himself of no reputation, taking the form of a bondservant, and coming in the likeness of men. And being found in appearance as a man, He humbled Himself and became obedient to the point of death, even the death of the cross (Philippians 2:6–8).

This little passage is packed with power; it contains a lot that we could consider. But Paul's point is that Christ took an uncommon descent. He left the privileges of heaven and became a Man—a Man who lived for others to the point of laying down His life for their sake. And it wasn't just any ordinary death that Christ experienced: it was death on a cross—which meant assuming the guilt of the whole world and being forsaken by God.

As I said, this is the lowest bow anyone has ever taken, or could ever. But it was almost as if Christ couldn't help Himself—which is, after all, what love and delight do to a person. Ideally, when two lives are joined together in marriage—which, as we discovered, is what Christ's ultimate goal is in this whole process—all sense of self is lost. Each person bows to the needs of the other. Yes, marriage is indeed a humbling experience, and since God delights in us and wants to enjoy full intimacy with us, He rejects all self-interest, lifting us and our well-being up, raising it over and above His own.

Interestingly, Jesus Himself points to the fact that His heart beats to the rhythm of humility, and His posture is that of bowing and bending to the needs of others. In His grand appeal for us to come to Him to find rest for our souls, He says that He is "meek and lowly in heart" (Matthew 11:29, KJV), or, as another version puts it, "gentle and *humble* in heart" (NASB; emphasis added). Though Christ and the Father have every right in the universe to be chest-thumping, Me-first egomaniacs, such behavior is the complete antithesis to what they're all about. Whereas we humans reach higher and higher still, God's heart sends Him lower and lower, that He might lift up the ones He ever delights in.

Notice how Carsten Johnsen puts it:

> True Christian love is revealed, not as a way of taking, but as a way of giving; not as a way of human pride, but as a way of divine humility.
>
> It may sound bold in the midst of a Greek-inspired culture to speak about the *humble* God. Throughout our lives we have imbibed the arch-pagan thought-forms of platonic idealism with all its vain-glorious insistence on climbing, climbing—in one's own power—to the stars. What glory could there be to us . . . in meekness? But it is God Himself who uses this description of Himself: "Learn of me. I am meek and lowly in heart." Matthew 11:29.[2]

Could it be that God's very essence is "divine humility"? Could it be that the almighty and all-powerful God of the Bible doesn't reveal His power through using brute force and demanding His own prerogatives, but precisely through His humility and bending down to be with us—all motivated by His love and delight in us?

A while back I shared this thought at one of my churches, and one of my parishioners came up to me afterward, wanting to speak with me. He told me, very gently and kindly, that he wasn't comfortable with the picture I was presenting of God. "You can say that God is humble, yes," he said, "but to propose that He would actually *bow* to us is a bit too much." Furthermore, in the sermon I had said that I would almost go so far as to say that God might even blush or get embarrassed when we heap praise upon Him, much like my dad does. He thought that in suggesting that, I was making God a little too much like a human being, as if God had feelings of inadequacy or inferiority, and he cautioned me not to get too carried away in how I described God's attitude.

I told him that I certainly wasn't meaning to attribute feelings of inadequacy to God, but then I pointed him to an example from Christ's life. "Didn't He kneel down at the feet of His disciples and wash their feet?" I asked. "And didn't Jesus say of Himself that He was 'meek and lowly in heart'?" My parishioner nodded in agreement but still couldn't seem to swallow in its entirety what I was saying.

A few months later I was reading one of my favorite books, and I came upon a few lines that I couldn't believe the author had written. "[Christ's] life was one of self-denial and thoughtful care for others. Every soul was precious in His eyes. While He ever bore Himself with divine dignity, *He bowed with the tenderest regard* to every member of the family of God. In all men He saw fallen souls whom it was His mission to save."[3]

When I read those words, I rejoiced that I wasn't the only one who proposed such a scandalous thought. I think the truth of the matter is that we become a bit uncomfortable with the idea that God is fully humble. We become uncomfortable with the thought that God descends lower and lower and lower. Doing that is completely antithetical to the human heart and behavior. We don't want a God who exemplifies humility; we want one who portrays pride and self-promotion, thus justifying our own natural tendency. But it's impossible for God to have those characteristics. He's omni-relational, and this inherently implies that His focus is outside of Himself, and His delight is in lifting others up—and simultaneously lowering Himself down.

The violinist

During the early morning rush hour a few years ago, a humble-looking young man in a Metro subway station in Washington, D.C., pulled out a violin and started to play. Since such "concerts" are common occurrences in the Metro stations of America's capital, as they are in many other cities around the world, few people paid much attention, and even fewer people threw coins into the young man's violin case, which was resting at his feet. The young man played on for forty-three minutes, performing six classical pieces. When his performance came to an anticlimactic end, he had collected all of thirty-two dollars, which had been contributed by about thirty of the thousand people who passed by him during that time.

A few months later, an article in *The Washington Post* revealed that the whole thing was an experiment. But not just any old experiment. The young man who had caught the attention of so few people was Joshua Bell, one of the greatest violinists in the world. Bell has performed for heads of state, and three nights before his performance in the Washington, D.C., Metro station, he had sold out a concert in Boston, where some of the cheaper tickets went for one hundred dollars each. The violin he played was handcrafted in 1713 by Antonio Stradivari and is worth roughly three and a half million dollars. And to top it all off, the songs he performed in the Metro station were some of the most challenging classical pieces in the world.

Yet few people had noticed. There was no applause and no

recognition—a point that made Bell nervous and embarrassed each time he ended a piece. This world-famous musician, who has played for presidents and kings, felt insecure about his reception. "When you play for ticket-holders," he explained later, "you are already validated. I have no sense [that] that I need to [work at being] accepted. I'm already accepted. Here, there was this thought: *What if they don't like me? What if they resent my presence?*"[4]

What a profound statement! "What if they resent my presence?" Make no mistake about it; God doesn't have an inferiority complex. He isn't insecure. But still, this loving and delighting omni-relational God has humbled Himself far more than Joshua Bell ever could. The violin He plays is worth a lot more than three and a half million million dollars. Not only has He had audiences with kings and queens and dignitaries the world over, but He is the One who actually created them. Could it be that while many of us worry about whether Christ will accept us, He nervously awaits our response, almost as if He's waiting to find out whether *we* will accept *Him*?

To that end, Christ—precisely because of His delighting heart—humbled Himself in a grand attempt to get us to accept Him once again. In bending down, He lifted us up. And so passionately has He pursued us that He bowed to the lowest point of the universe.

We'll explore the implications of that in the next few chapters. In the meantime, we can thoughtfully reflect upon our attitude toward the posture that God has assumed. Are we going to be even more insensitive than those subway riders and ignore the One who *created* music—and us?

CHAPTER ELEVEN

THE CUP

I can't figure out how to start this chapter. I've been delaying writing for a few days now. It seems as if whatever I come up with falls infinitely short. Much of it sounds cheap. Funny anecdotes and clever stories just don't seem to do the present topic justice.

Why?

Because it is one of the most sacred and profound subjects the Bible presents. To me, it's the apex of the whole biblical record. When Moses approached the burning bush, God told him to take off his sandals because he was on holy ground. This topic seems to demand the same kind of respect—only exponentially more. I'm not sure how anyone can encounter the picture of God we are about to see without being gripped emotionally. Time and time again, when I linger upon this awe-inspiring narrative, I am overwhelmed by a multiplicity of reactions—guilt, pity, gratitude, amazement. I hope you will be stirred as well.

"I come to the garden alone . . ."

It's very sobering to see this picture of God. Quite literally, words almost cannot express the profound mystery that surrounds the scene. And yet it is there. It is undeniable. The great mystery of all mysteries is that this omni-relational God, in the person of Jesus, finds Himself at a place where every single relationship He has ever known and enjoyed is sadly deteriorating.

Can you see Him?

Can you hear Him?

Here He is in the Garden of Gethsemane,* which stood just outside the walls of Jerusalem. Jesus has come here many times before. He has often gone to His knees, gaining strength from His heavenly Father through hours in prayer. But this time, strangely, the opposite seems to be happening. Rather than gaining strength from His encounter with His Father, His strength seems to be diminishing.

And He's alone.

He's not supposed to be alone, but He is. Jesus, who is energized by relationships, invited Peter, James, and John to be with Him during this most trying moment. He was hoping that they would be an encouragement to Him. But though these three, His closest earthly companions, are just a stone's throw away from Him, they seem to be a universe away. So, when He expresses His feelings in words such as "My soul is exceedingly sorrowful, even unto death" (Matthew 26:38, KJV), a strange silence envelops His companions. Instead of offering Him a word of encouragement or even inquiring about what's happening, they direct their attention to finding a place where they can nap for a few minutes.

So Jesus struggles on alone.

It would be terrible for us to move along without meditating upon the statement that the disciples neglected, however. We can't afford to pass quickly over what Jesus said. To some of us, the statement may seem rote. We've read it a million times and think we've milked it for all its theological value. Others may have never encountered this statement before and don't recognize anything profound or valuable in it. But it has incredible depth and affords insight deep

---

Gethsemane is an Aramaic term that means "oil press." The generally accepted view is that there were olive trees in this garden and a press for extracting oil from the olives.

into the heart of our omni-relational God.

To begin with, we need to make sure we understand what Jesus was talking about when He said His "soul" was exceedingly sorrowful. In the Greek in which this statement was originally written, the word translated "soul" is *psuchē.* It's the source of the English word *psyche,* and it has to do with our emotional state. So when Jesus says that His *psuchē* "is exceedingly sorrowful," He is speaking about His emotional—and we might even say spiritual—state. Evidently, there is something going on within His soul that is causing Him great anxiety.

So serious does this psychological conflict become that Luke tells us Jesus' sweat actually became like "great drops of blood" (Luke 22:44, NKJV). This was no ordinary struggle. I've been emotionally distraught, but I've never come to the point where I was perspiring so heavily that my sweat was like great drops of blood. An infinitely heavy burden had been laid upon Jesus.

Immortal souls?

But there's another component to Jesus' statement about His psyche that we need to ponder too. He proclaimed that His "soul is exceedingly sorrowful, even unto death."

"Wait a minute, Jesus," we ask. "Are You saying that both Your soul and every other soul can die? Aren't souls immortal?"

Apparently not. In fact, the overwhelming testimony of Scripture is that the soul isn't a discreet entity independent of the individual person. As Anglican bishop and New Testament scholar N. T. Wright points out, "The idea that every human possesses an immortal soul, which is the 'real' part of them, finds little support in the Bible."[1] Instead, the Bible presents the idea that the soul is the whole person, a combination of all the properties that make up human beings. This is why some versions of the Bible translate *psuchē* as "life." They do so because the "soul" is essentially the total package of all that life consists of—the body, the mind, and the breath of life.

This realization multiplies by a hundredfold the significance of

Jesus' struggle. Elsewhere, the apostle John—who, though sleeping at the time, was right there with Jesus—informs us that Jesus "laid down His life for us" (1 John 3:16). The word translated "life" is the same word we encountered in the Garden. So not only does Jesus take upon Himself an incredible psychological weight, but He actually lays down His very soul. John informs us that this is how "we know love" (Ibid.).

Pause for a second and contemplate what this implies. Here, in the Garden, Jesus is actually facing total annihilation. It isn't the death of His temporal body that He is dreading. And believe it or not, other people have suffered greater physical pain than Jesus is about to encounter, so He isn't sweating drops like blood because He is dreading the whip of the Roman soldiers or even the nails that will be driven through His hands. All that, though definitely painful, will last only a few hours; and, if it were true that He would really continue to exist—in heaven, maybe—after His physical life is taken from Him, then a few hours of torture would certainly pale in comparison to the reunion with His Father He was about to experience.

But Jesus is really agonizing in the Garden. He's facing the real possibility of undergoing something never yet experienced—total annihilation.

Early on in His ministry Jesus told His disciples, "Do not fear those who kill the body but cannot kill the soul" (Matthew 10:28). In other words, He was encouraging them not to worry about those who could inflict physical and temporal pain—even death—upon them. Such people couldn't rob them of eternal life. "Rather," Jesus declared, "fear Him who is able to destroy both soul and body in hell" (Ibid.).

This is what Jesus is facing in the Garden. In a few short hours, the Roman soldiers will lay into Him with their full fury. This is why He cries out three times, "O My Father, if it is possible, let this cup pass from Me" (Matthew 26:39).

There can be no doubt what Jesus is referring to when He talks about the "cup." Perhaps there is no more clear-cut connection between a metaphorical allusion that Jesus used and the Old Testament. The psalmists and prophets repeatedly spoke of a "cup" that God was reserving for a specific group of people. "In the hand of the Lord," Asaph wrote, "there is a cup, and the wine is red; it is fully mixed, and He pours it out; surely its dregs shall all the wicked of the earth drain and drink down" (Psalm 75:8). And Isaiah declared that God took "the cup of trembling, the dregs of the cup of My fury" out of Israel's hand and placed it in the hands of those who afflicted them (Isaiah 51:22). In other words, this cup to which Jesus refers is reserved for the wicked. It contains God's wrath. It is the "wages of sin" that Paul speaks of (Romans 6:23). It is the "reward" that those who refuse to give up sin and to have a relationship with God are to receive. And in the Garden, it is being placed in Jesus' hand.

No wonder it is called the "cup of trembling." Jesus can barely hold it in His quivering, sweat-soaked hands. As He lies face down on the ground, sweating drops like blood, He is commencing the journey to hell. This is why He pleads with His Father three times to take the cup from Him. Bearing the full weight of His Father's fury upon sin just about kills Him. But each time He asks for release, He also prays that His Father's will for His life and death be played out.

Sleeping

Something else of interest is going on in this garden. Peter, James, and John are sleeping. The irony of this plot twist is unfortunate to the nth degree. Just a short time before, James and John's mother had come to Jesus, begging that He place her two sons beside Him when He set up His kingdom.

"You do not know what you ask," Jesus responded to her and to her two sons—who, no doubt, had put her up to it. And then He asked them a very pointed and sobering question, "Are you able to drink the cup that I am about to drink?" (Matthew 20:22).

The two nodded their heads vigorously in the affirmative, assuring

Jesus that they were up to the task. But they weren't. When Jesus needed them most, when He sweated drops like blood and pleaded with His Father for His life, He found them sleeping. We must not miss or underestimate the importance of this point. This omni-relational Jesus, who was about to drink the cup of God's fury, longed to have someone with whom He could share it. This is not to say that, as some kind of co-redeemers, the three disciples in the Garden with Jesus were to lift part of the load and help pay the price for the salvation of the world. No mortal can contribute one iota to his or her own salvation, or to anyone else's. But that wasn't what Jesus wanted. What He eagerly hoped His disciples would do at that time was to comfort and encourage Him in His sufferings. That would have energized Him, assured Him that His journey to hell would not be in vain.

Later, the apostles would pick up on this theme and admonish their audiences to "rejoice" when they were able to "share" or "participate" in "Christ's sufferings" (see Romans 8:17; 1 Peter 4:13). Doing so produces an intimacy with Jesus that is unequaled.

Of course, even in the absence of any encouragement from His disciples, love ultimately prevailed, and Jesus resolved to go to the cross. But that was because God had to resort to plan B. When the disciples failed Jesus, God sent an angel in place of them to encourage and strengthen Him.

Here's the sobering reality: all of us must drink from the same cup that Jesus drank from there in the Garden. As I said previously, this doesn't mean that we earn our own salvation. It doesn't mean that we pay the price for our own sins. Nevertheless, we are all invited to drink from that same cup and share in Christ's sufferings. To paraphrase an old and wonderful hymn, "Must Jesus drink from the cup alone and all the world go free? No, there's a cup for everyone, and there's a cup for me."

How do I know?

Interestingly, there is one other metaphorical usage of the word *cup* in the Old Testament that takes a different slant than that of the aforementioned verses. I think it offers an interesting insight on this whole discussion.

Psalm of trauma

In Psalm 116, we read a very poignant reflection that an unnamed writer shared. We don't know the exact circumstances surrounding the creation of that psalm, but its author was apparently experiencing a lot of emotional and psychological trauma. "The pains of death surrounded me," he wrote, "and the pangs of Sheol laid hold of me" (Psalm 116:3).

I believe this last phrase gives us a little insight into who this unnamed author was. Sheol is another name for hell. In fact, the King James Version translates the verse this way. So, the author of the passage has been grabbed by the throes of hell. Then, at the end of the psalm, he announces, "I will pay my vows to the LORD now in the presence of all His people, in the courts of the LORD's house, in the midst of you, O Jerusalem" (verses 18, 19).

This is a Messianic psalm. It gives us special insight into the emotional and spiritual battle that Jesus was fighting in the shadows of the Cross. It opens our understanding to the trauma that He experienced as Calvary loomed. It shows us the tremendous conflict going on within His psyche. He felt the clutches of eternal extinction tightening on Him, and He struggled, by faith, to hold on to His Father's promise of ultimate deliverance. Thus, He proclaims, "For You have delivered my soul from death" (verse 8). This statement was as much a prophecy as it was an accomplishment.

Our attention gravitates to the middle of the psalm. There, after wrestling with this tension between his own safety and the promised deliverance, with a heart full of love and gratitude, the psalmist poses the question, "What shall I render to the LORD for all His benefits toward me?" (verse 12). Then, with little hesitation, he answers his own question: "I will take up the cup" (verse 13).

There's that cup again! But there's more to it than simply "the cup." This cup has a label. It contains something. The keen observer would surmise that the psalmist is going to take up the cup of God's fury, but such a conclusion would be wrong. The cup doesn't contain God's wrath. No, indeed! The psalmist proclaims that he will "take up the cup of salvation."

Of course, there is no distinction between the cup of God's fury and the cup of salvation. They are one and the same. As Jesus drank the dregs of God's fury, He simultaneously filled the cup of the salvation of the world. And as we noted earlier, what Jesus began in Gethsemane and brought to completion on Calvary gave every human being the gift of life. We live today because Jesus lifted that cup to His lips and swallowed. By taking on Himself the wages of sin, He has also secured the gift of salvation for every human being. He suffered for every sinner—paid the price so all who wish to can enter God's eternal kingdom.

So, whether or not we realize it, you and I have benefited from Jesus' sacrifice. We're living and breathing because He drank from the cup. Yet there's still more. If we are to truly experience life—I mean *truly,* in all of its fullness—we must drink from that cup too.

Did you catch that? Those who have come to trust Jesus fully for their salvation are those who are willing to follow Him wherever He leads—even if that means drinking from His cup and participating in His sufferings. After all, this is what true relationship is all about. If we're going to respond to this omni-relational God, His experiences must become our experiences, His sufferings, our sufferings. However, we must always keep in mind that He has already paid the full price for our salvation, and our sharing in His sufferings doesn't mean that we're now reimbursing Him. We'll never have the resources to do that. We'll always be indebted to Him.

But casting our lot with Him ultimately *does* mean being treated as He was treated. And when we share in His sufferings, we love and appreciate Him even more. To this end, I am reminded of what one thoughtful writer has said. "Of all the gifts that Heaven can bestow upon men," she wrote, "fellowship with Christ in His sufferings is the most weighty trust and the highest honor."[2] After all, life and salvation are truly all about responding to the omni-relational God of the universe when He invites us to join our hearts *completely* to His. They are about participating in everything He does.

As we observe Jesus in the Garden, we realize just how far He has extended Himself in pursuit of us. We see Him as the God who is everlasting but who was willing to become the God who is nevermore. Then, do our hearts not overflow with gratitude and awe, asking Him, "Can I *truly* have the privilege of enjoying complete fellowship with You?"

His ever-longing heart of love hopes that is our response.

CHAPTER TWELVE

GOD IS DEAD

Many people have tried to kill God. It all started with that malicious fellow known as the devil—the one who tried to undermine and then to usurp God's authority; the one whom Christ described as a "murderer from the beginning" (John 8:44). Friedrich Nietzsche, the nineteenth-century German philosopher, infamously declared "God is dead . . . and we have killed him." Though Nietzsche's declaration was a little premature, it betrays the underlying belief he harbored: that humankind would be better off without God. This sentiment has appeared over and over again since the dawn of creation.

Of course, we need to be cautious here lest we start patting ourselves on the back, believing that we're exceptions. Truth be told, we are all born with the craving to push self forward at all costs. That's called *pride*. No human being who has entered the world has been immune to such thinking, no matter how little "self-esteem" he or she has. And if pride were allowed to have its way, it would eliminate God altogether. "Down in its heart of hearts," writes psychologist William Backus, "our pride generates lethal animosity *against God* and promotes the belief that 'I ought to be, can be, and by right *am* my own god.' *Every* person's proud heart, in some way or in every way, wants to be in charge, wants to displace God and move into primacy, taking first place."[1]

Recognizing this reality makes Jesus' struggle in Gethsemane all the more remarkable. It makes His constant pursuit of us all the more amazing as well. Just think of it! God is expending an infinite amount of energy in an attempt to pursue and redeem and bring back into complete relationship with Himself a group of people who are trying to eliminate Him. That's simply mind-boggling to me.

Yet here is something perhaps even more remarkable. In a grand attempt to pursue and redeem us, God actually allowed His Son to suffer the very fate that you and I wanted for Him. He surrendered Him to death!

What God did stands in stark contrast to the way we operate. If we know someone is trying to eliminate us, we run the other way, or we set up a barricade and go down fighting.

Not God. In fact, a short time before His death, Jesus shared a very interesting insight into His whole mode of operation. "No one can take My life from Me," He declared (John 10:18, NLT). This is a simple, incontrovertible fact because Jesus is God, and God inherently possesses immortality. Thus, we're no more likely to be able to kill God than to be able to empty the ocean with a spoon.

But in fact, as I noted in the last chapter, it wasn't really any of the physical torments Jesus suffered that brought about His death. The Roman soldiers and the spitting throng didn't really end His life. It seems unbelievable, but it's true: Jesus poignantly declared that He Himself would actually sacrifice His life voluntarily (see John 10:18); He would willingly lay it down. Jesus voluntarily suffered under the hand of the Almighty God—the only way that His life could end. Indeed, it is on the cross of Calvary that we witness the voluntary death of God.

The cross

When the time had finally come for Jesus to go to the cross and complete His earthly mission, He went to the Garden and prayed an agonizing prayer. Then a band of hooligans—along with Judas, one of His twelve disciples—came and seized Him. They dragged Him before Caiaphas, the chief priest, where He was questioned by the elders of His own people. After great physical and verbal abuse, He was carted off to Pontius Pilate, who also questioned Him and then sent Him to Herod. Each of these officials had the opportunity to free the innocent Jesus but decided not to. The pressure from the crowd and the craving to please the leaders of the Jews no doubt made them hesitant to excuse Him. Ultimately, the desires to preserve self and to eliminate God sprang forth from the hearts of these cowardly men.

In the process, Jesus was whipped; He was beaten; His beard was plucked out; and a thorny crown was placed on His head and a splintery cross on His back, and He was led to a hill called Golgotha—the "place of a skull." However, as we said before, these tortures hardly fazed Him. Two things eclipsed any notice of the physical torment that He was suffering: an almost insurmountable anxiety caused by His Father's withdrawing His presence from Him, and, perhaps just as significantly, His feeling that no one cared about what He was doing.

That second perception is a cold, harsh reality that is relevant to our own lives. God forbid that we ever find ourselves in the position occupied by some of Jesus' closest and most trusted followers when Jesus craved their companionship the most. Peter had sworn that he never could and never would deny Jesus—and then he did, three times. James and John, who vowed that they could drink from the same cup Jesus was about to drink from, slept soundly while Jesus pleaded with His heavenly Father in the Garden. Jesus' other disciples fled when He was arrested, and one of them actually ran away naked, so determined was he to escape (see Mark 14:51, 52). And perhaps worst of all, another of Jesus' disciples, Judas, sold Him into the hands of the leaders of the Jews for thirty pieces of silver! Though thirty pieces of silver could buy a lot of real estate, putting a price tag on the infinitely valuable Son of God is staggering in its hubris.

It's no wonder, then, that Jesus became increasingly discouraged as He went to Golgotha. He had worked with these twelve men for three and a half years, desperately trying to bring them into full and complete relationship with Himself—only to have them turn their backs on Him when He needed them the most. Would they ever get it? Would they ever realize and appreciate that He was going to the cross to fulfill His divine mission of pursuing them to the farthest depths of existence—and beyond that, to non-existence? And if the disciples—men who knew Jesus well, who had lived with Him through those three and a half years—were overlooking His mind-boggling pursuit, how could He hope that anyone else ever would notice and respond to it?

But what really overwhelmed the heart of Jesus even to the point of death was the realization that He was pursuing the members of the human race at the cost of carrying their guilt upon His shoulders, guilt that ultimately separated Him from His Father, who ever and always before had enjoyed an omni-relational existence with Him.

The story behind the story

As we discovered in the last chapter, we encounter incredible insight into the experience of Jesus when we meditate upon Psalms. While the four Gospel books—Matthew, Mark, Luke, and John—narrate for us a third-person account of Jesus' life, death, and resurrection, the book of Psalms almost seems to serve as a behind-the-scenes diary that alerts us to Jesus' emotional state during these experiences. And it's no wonder. Biblical scholars posit that those who penned Psalms must have been given special insight that enabled them to describe both their personal struggles and Jesus' sufferings.[2]

Thus, when David writes, "My heart is severely pained within me, and the terrors of death have fallen upon me" (Psalm 55:4), he not only tells us his own plight, but he also paints a poignant picture of Jesus' horrific Golgotha experience. So it is no wonder that as Jesus hung naked on Calvary's cross, David's gut-wrenching question,

"My God, My God, why have You forsaken me?" escaped from His lips (see Psalm 22:1).

Of course, this is more than simply a connection meaningful only to academics. These two passages—Psalm 22 and Psalm 55—give us a commentary on the full measure of Jesus' agony. Psalm 22 reveals Jesus as He feels forsaken, alone, naked, as unvalued as a worm, disregarded by the whole human race, and, worse, as vulnerable before God as wax is to fire.

But in Psalm 55, Jesus declares something quite intriguing—something that seems almost unbelievable. After explaining that He is "severely pained," He takes a surprising turn and declares,

> It is not an enemy who reproaches me; then I could bear it. Nor is it one who hates me who has exalted himself against me; then I could hide from him. But it was you, a man my equal, my companion and my acquaintance. We took sweet counsel together, and walked to the house of God in the throng (Psalm 55:12–14).

Many people suppose that when Jesus spoke of His opponent here, He was referring to Judas Iscariot—the one who betrayed Him for thirty pieces of silver. While this may be a perfectly legitimate interpretation, it seems possible that Jesus felt betrayed by a much more unlikely antagonist—none other than His own heavenly Father. Here's the evidence. In this psalm, Jesus shifts from the third person to the second person, speaking of a "you" who has turned his back on Him. The book of Psalms uses the Hebrew word that is here translated "you" 117 other times, and *in every single one of those instances, "you" refers to God.* In fact, just a few verses later in this same psalm, the psalmist again uses the Hebrew word translated "you," and it unambiguously refers to God (see verse 23).

Thus, what we see here is startling. Jesus and the Father have enjoyed companionship, fellowship, and friendship together from eternity past. They have taken the joyous journey together to the heavenly sanctuary, time and again enjoying sweet counsel. They lived and breathed and cried together. Yet now, right here on Golgotha, something unimaginable is happening—something so foreign to Jesus' psyche that He can hardly even comprehend it. He feels as though His own Father actually hates Him. He feels as if His Father is reproaching Him, or even taunting Him. He simply cannot bear it.

What's going on?

Fortunately, where the psalmists leave us short, the apostle Paul comes along and puts the matter in theological terms: "He [God] made Him [Jesus] who knew no sin to be sin for us" (2 Corinthians 5:21). And "Christ has redeemed us from the curse of the law, *having become a curse for us*" (Galatians 3:13; emphasis added). God, the Father, placed upon Jesus' shoulders the guilt of the entire human race. Quite literally, He was blamed for every sin that has ever been committed—every rape, murder, lie, and hate-filled word. It's as if all of us collectively sinned and then pointed to Jesus and said, "He did it." And despite His innocence, He didn't point His finger back at us and say, "No, no. They did it!" Instead, in effect, He said, "You're right."

"It's all your fault!"

The analogy I am about to use almost seems sacrilegious, but it's about as close as I can come to giving us a glimpse of how Jesus must have felt. I remember going to a college hockey game a few years ago and being startled by the hostility displayed—even though I had been to many hockey games before and knew the brutality involved. During this particular game, whenever the opposing team would allow a goal, three thousand fans would point their index fingers at the goalie and yell in unison, "It's all your fault! It's all your fault! It's all your fault!"

I suppose an athlete who played at that level would probably have learned how to tune out such banter. But just the same, I can't imagine that it would be very easy for a twenty-one- or twenty-two-year-old to bear it. Despite what we learned growing up, some words actually *do* hurt us. When people mock or jeer us, it *does* affect our psyche. I know that when I have messed up or done something wrong in a room full of people—or even in front of just a handful of them—I want to crawl into a hole.

Jesus felt the collective gaze of the entire universe bearing down upon Him. But most important—and, as I said, the hockey analogy almost makes me feel disrespectful—He felt as though His Father disapproved of Him. The feeling that God had forsaken Him, that He despised Him, yes, even hated Him, overwhelmed Jesus. He had the acute sense that His Father was pointing His divine finger down at Him and saying, "It's all your fault!"

Of course, as I've noted previously, sin cannot remain in the presence of God without producing dire consequences for the one who is bearing that sin, so something big happened on Golgotha. Something beyond our comprehension. We know that Jesus felt that His Father had abandoned Him. But we don't know for sure whether His Father did, in fact, withdraw His presence, or whether Jesus merely felt that the Father had done so. Nor can we quite figure out whether God visited the full weight of sin's penalty on His Son, or whether Jesus' death was self-induced, the result of feeling overwhelmed with grief to the point of death—what we so often call "dying of a broken heart."

Most likely, both of these things happened. There, on Calvary, God rained down His vengeance upon sin, while at the same time, Jesus was engulfed by an incredible sense of guilt, and both were the death of Him—indeed, the death of God.

But we do know the crux of the matter: Jesus' pursuit of us took Him to the lowest depths of the universe. Jesus—as God Himself—could have merely pursued us to the point of taking on human flesh. That would have been unbelievable enough. He could have pursued us a step further by becoming a lonely Man on the dusty roads of Palestine, and that itself would have been incomprehensible. He could have pursued us all the way to Pilate's courtyard and suffered there the lashes applied by the Roman soldiers and the jeers of the mocking crowd. This would have been unfathomable to the nth degree. He could even have pursued us to Calvary and allowed His hands to be brutally nailed to a dead tree and a crown of thorns to be thrust upon His head. That would have been inexplicable.

But He went further.

He went infinitely further.

He pursued us all the way to hell—without the hope of ever returning.

At this point it would be tempting to say that He did all this without batting an eyelash. But saying that would be more than merely understating the case; it would be casting contempt upon the infinite suffering that Jesus experienced on our behalf, to save the lost world.

Many have proposed that Jesus willingly laid down His life for us so that He could someday enjoy a full relationship with us throughout eternity, and since He is an omni-relational being, that would certainly be true of Him. But here's the really amazing thing: As Jesus hung on the cross, He feared that after He drew His last breath He would never live again. Hope for Himself, for His future, didn't present itself to Him that fateful Friday afternoon. Yet His primary concern was not about Himself or His loss. No, what carried Him forward that day was the realization that by His death He would be able to accomplish something life-changing for us—and for His Father. He was willing to secure our salvation by dying in our place *so that His Father—who also is omni-relational—would be able to enjoy an eternal relationship with us!*

This is the self-abandonment that drove our Savior.

This is how far grace will pursue.

CHAPTER THIRTEEN

THE ENDLESS PURSUIT

A lot is made of so-called deathbed confessions. While I'm writing this, Christopher Hitchens, one of the most well-known atheist evangelists, is battling with terminal cancer. He insists that if he were to have a "coming to the Lord" experience on his deathbed, we should assume that he no longer has all his faculties.

Richard Dawkins, one of Hitchens's cohorts in the fight against God, has even gone so far as to say that he wants to have someone record his final moments so no one can claim he turned to God before drawing his final breath.[1] These men have done this because many people have claimed that influential atheists—like Charles Darwin—have been converted on their deathbeds, and the possibility of people saying this about them has not sat well with those who have taken up Darwin's mantle.

Whether or not the likes of Hitchens, Dawkins, or Darwin have had or will have a conversion at death's door is not the point, however. The fact that we know of people who have legitimately surrendered their lives to Christ in their final seconds shows a significant reality. At the beginning of this book, we noted the biblical statement that goodness and mercy "pursue" us, but at that point we didn't take time to dwell upon the next clause of the verse, which declares that God's goodness, love, mercy, and grace will pursue us *all the days of our lives* (see Psalm 23:6).

This reality is quite remarkable. It also is quite exhaustive. Even though it might sound like a cliché, God is on a 24/7 pursuit of us. He works from sunup to sundown trying to draw us into relationship with Himself. He never gives up on us, not for one second. From the moment we draw life's first breath until we surrender our last, He is continuously on our trail. Every day of our lives God knocks on the door of our hearts seeking a relationship with us. Every second of every day of our entire lives is filled with loving invitations from God to surrender to His almost irresistible wooing. In fact, the Bible even hints at the idea that this pursuit starts *before* we're born—at least that was the case with the prophet Jeremiah, to whom God said, "Before I formed you in the womb I knew you; before you were born I sanctified you; I ordained you a prophet to the nations" (Jeremiah 1:5). It's no wonder, then, that we hear our hearts crying for something more than anything we can obtain apart from God. It's no wonder that the Tom Bradys and Boris Beckers of the world never find satisfaction when they've set their aspirations on things other than God.

And God doesn't discontinue His pursuit of us when we turn Him away once or twice—or a thousand times. He doesn't stop with a dozen Nos or a hundred Go aways. Don't get me wrong; He isn't going to be annoying about it. But He ever sweetly entreats us to say Yes to His overtures, and He'll continue to do so until our dying day.

"On a hill far away . . ."

Christ's last few moments on the cross provide a very interesting demonstration of this very reality. Luke tells us that "there were also two others, criminals," who were to be put to death with Him (Luke 23:32). We don't know much about either of the men crucified with Him; and what we do know is kind of a mixed bag. One of the two eventually said Yes to Jesus. Luke wrote only three verses about him, but perhaps we can use a little bit of our "sanctified imagination" and speculate about this young man's life.

He was, no doubt, born to a Jewish family. We don't know whether his parents were pious or were lukewarm about their faith. Whatever the case, somewhere along the line his life took a turn for the worse and he became a hardened criminal. It didn't happen overnight, of course. It never does. It started with a little stealing, a tiny fib, but it ultimately grew to grand theft.

Time and time again this man felt convicted that he needed to give up his criminal ways. He knew he was playing with fire, but far too often he'd been able to evade the law. So, whenever the conviction came, he listened to the wily lies of the devil and bought into the falsehoods that he would never get caught, that he didn't need to give it up, that even if he wanted to, he couldn't. After all, this was now his way of life.

His world was really shaken, though, when a man named Jesus happened to be in the same locale where he was planning one of his heists. He would be scoping out a neighborhood when all of a sudden a massive throng would come barreling down the streets, hailing this Man and singing His praises. Jesus was healing people and proclaiming something He called the gospel, the "good news." A few times he actually made eye contact with Him, and he felt an undeniable connection. It was almost as if he felt the yearning for him that was in Jesus' heart—as if Jesus could reach down into the depths of his soul, read his thoughts, and stir his inner being.

These brief encounters with Jesus left the thief very upset. For days after seeing Him, he was anxious and even depressed. He couldn't shake this Man's incontrovertible ability to appeal to his heart as if He were pleading for him to give up his life and respond wholeheartedly to His appeals. But, as many so often do, he tried to silence the invitation; he tried to shake off the unspoken pleas. And when he had endured days of not being able to get Jesus out of his mind, he would drown his anxiety with alcohol, hoping that it would numb the stirring of his heart.

After a while he was able to forget this Man altogether. He was able to silence his conscience. But not forever.

One day, something very strange happened. Up till that day the thief had always been able to outrun the authorities, but not this time. He couldn't figure out how they happened to catch him. It was almost as if there was a conspiracy, as if someone was working behind the scenes, orchestrating his arrest. If so, whoever was on his trail must have been pursuing him for a long time. Whatever the case, he found himself in court with little hope. The authorities had a whole list of charges against him. As they went down the list one by one, he had very little to say in his own defense. They had the goods on him.

Then the verdict came down: he was to be executed, and before he knew it, he was carrying a cross up a hill outside the walls of Jerusalem. He understood the full implications of this. When he was a child, his mother had taught him what Scripture said, and he remembered full well that anyone who was hanged on a tree was considered to be under God's curse. So he believed that there was no hope for him, that his eternal fate was sealed.

As he slowly plodded up that steep path, he tried to come to grips with his destiny. He realized that he had caused a great deal of pain, but he also knew that he was the product of a difficult past, that he had never been dealt a fair hand. Resentment grew in his heart as he tried to justify what he'd done, and anger filled him as he looked at the soldiers who were leading him to his tragic end. He knew that these savage men were not a whole lot better than he, yet he was about to be tortured to death, while the civil authorities paid these men to be what they were.

Crucified

When the thief reached the place of crucifixion, they laid him on the splintered wood of the crossbeam and bound his hands to it. Then, with a few strong blows, a soldier drove an iron nail through one of his hands. He tried to be brave, but he couldn't help himself—he screamed out in agony. And with each subsequent nail, his anger toward his executioners grew.

Then, through his bloody tears, he noticed something unbelievable. One of the men being crucified with him—someone whom he knew from his life of crime—was also letting out blood-curdling screams, and he was struggling with his executioners. But to his amazement, he noticed that the Man between himself and the other criminal wasn't even whimpering as the soldiers drove the nails through His hands.

When the soldiers raised the three crosses off the ground, the thief had a better look at the Man in the middle. He knew he had seen Him before—when and where he couldn't remember. Though he was suffering incredible pain, for the next few minutes his mind raced through his memories. He was determined to figure out who this Man was and where he had seen Him before.

While he searched his memories, he kept an eye on the mystery Man. The thief soon realized that this Man was no ordinary criminal. In fact, He was no ordinary man. Just about everyone who came to Golgotha that day had some kind of opinion about Him. Some pitied Him, but the majority laughed and mocked and jeered Him.

What the criminal saw made him wonder what this Man had done to cause such visceral and impassioned reactions. What little he'd seen of Him carried an overwhelming aura of innocence. His face seemed to glow with an indisputable humility. His lips, though quivering a little now, spoke of grace. And His eyes . . . no matter where His eyes roamed, they seemed filled with compassion for every person they rested on.

As the criminal hung there, watching this unusual Man, he noticed His gaze settle upon the small group of soldiers who had just nailed Him to the cross. For some reason, they stood close to the middle cross as they gambled over the Man's clothing, laughing carelessly as they cast their lots.

What the criminal heard next was almost unbelievable, yet it was life-changing. No, it was death-changing. Mustering up all the strength He could, this Man in the middle drew a deep breath and then cried out with tears in His voice, "Father, forgive them, for they do not know what they do" (Luke 23:34).

Then all that the criminal had seen and heard of this extraordinary Man came rushing into his consciousness. The admiring throngs. The healings. The cries of "hosanna." The messages of compassion and love. And most of all, the quick yet heart-piercing glances the Man had directed at him as he walked by—looks that he was unable to shake until he drowned them. And at that precise moment, the criminal realized that this Man was the Messiah.

And here the Messiah was, hanging on a "tree" as a condemned criminal, forever under the curse of a God He called "Father." It didn't make sense. It made absolutely no sense.

But then, as the thief looked back in his mind's eye, and as he looked up at the sign above Jesus' head—the sign that read, "The King of the Jews"—it all began to make sense. The biblical prophecies he remembered from his childhood began to fall into place. This Man was dying to save humanity.

He began to wonder, *Is it possible that He might be dying for me?* And he began to flirt with the idea that maybe, just maybe, there was still hope for him. Yes, in the past he had blown opportunity after opportunity—second chances, third chances . . . zillionth chances. But a barely remembered passage of Scripture penned by a man who hailed from the same tiny town as Jesus kept running through his mind: "Surely goodness and mercy shall pursue me *all the days of my life*" (Psalm 23:6; my wording). Then the thought occurred to him that perhaps Jesus was fulfilling this passage before his very eyes. Perhaps this was Jesus' primary mission. Maybe He had come all the way to the cross just to save him—hardened criminal that he was.

So, not wanting to pass up this last opportunity before he drew his last breath, he worked up the strength to frantically blurt out a very unpolished request. He'd had no chance to rehearse this prayer, but it was the best he could manage. "Lord," he said, "remember me when You come into Your kingdom." With little hesitation, Jesus turned His head and fixed His gaze upon the man. There were those eyes—those deep, dark eyes that had longingly appealed to his heart.

And for the first time ever, Jesus verbalized the results of His overtures to this man, replying, "Assuredly, I say to you today, you will be with Me in Paradise."*

Though condemned as a criminal and now hung upon a cross to die, the man could hardly believe his good fortune. For the first time in his life a sense of peace enveloped him. The first 99.99 percent of his life had been filled with anxiety, consternation, and agony, but now, in the eleventh hour, he was filled with an overwhelming joy. He was going to experience eternity with the Man who had pursued him all the way to the cross!

Eternal security

Something about the last-second conversion the criminal experienced has always intrigued me. I've pondered this little story time and again, and each time it has struck me as interesting that this criminal is one of very few, out of all the people who have ever lived, that we *know* beyond a shadow of a doubt will be in heaven when we get there. Think about it. We know Enoch is there. We know Moses and Elijah are there. We know an unnumbered throng—perhaps twenty-four—who were resurrected when Jesus was, are there. But no one else in all of Scripture has a place there now.

This fortunate fellow, this former thief, isn't there yet. But he received something else. He's the only person mentioned in the Bible to whom Jesus said, "Assuredly, . . . you will be . . . in Paradise."

That's kind of mind blowing, if you ask me. I'm not, of course, saying that the likes of David, John, or Paul had no assurance of salvation. But I find it irresistibly interesting that one of the most hardened criminals in all of Scripture was the only person to whom God *promised* salvation—the only one who knew *for sure* where he was heading upon death.

---

*There were no punctuation marks in the original documents of the Bible. Long after Luke wrote this verse, someone put a comma before the word *today*. I've put it after that word instead, which makes this verse harmonize with what the rest of Scripture says about life after death.

Of course, it speaks to God's gracious pursuit of this man, and it testifies to His unrelenting love. Perhaps some of this man's loved ones who outlived him were able to read this account. Suppose you were his brother or his mother or wife and you hadn't gone to his execution and had never heard about what happened there. Imagine, then, receiving a copy of Luke's account forty years later and reading this gripping tale. This loved one of yours had made a full surrender to Jesus after all! And there's no doubt about where he'd spend eternity.

On the other hand, I wonder how many people will be utterly shocked to see this man in heaven. But shocked or not, they'll be excited—and they'll know that he got there the same way they did—by responding to the appeals of the omni-relational God, who pursued them all the days of their lives.

And us? We aren't promised tomorrow. We don't know when we'll die. But we *are* promised that God will pursue us relentlessly through every today and tomorrow we have.

Perhaps you have sensed His tugging at your heart but have never surrendered to Him. Perhaps you've tried to bury that tugging under life's distractions and have just now sensed that you need to begin eternity now—that you have ignored the invitations and spurned the appeals for too long.

Why not, like that nameless criminal, respond to Christ's overtures and give yourself—all you are and all you have—to Him forever?

CHAPTER FOURTEEN

VALUE

I hate to say it, but many times when my wife comes home from a shopping trip and excitedly shows me what she has bought, she is disappointed in my half-hearted, glazed-eye response. We each have a monthly allowance that we can spend on whatever we want, so it's not that I'm upset that she has made the purchase—it's just that I'm puzzled. The things she values and buys are not what I value or buy— and the reverse is true as well.

Of course, the world of eBay has left us all scratching our heads over what people buy, and what they pay for their "treasures." A quick Internet search of some of the craziest eBay purchases produces results that stagger us: a Doritos chip that looks like the pope's hat; a UFO detector; a jar that supposedly contains a ghost that was found in a cemetery. All these things sold. For real money.

Perhaps the most infamous eBay purchase was the grilled cheese sandwich that just happened to have an image burned into it that supposedly looked like the virgin Mary. What was the winning bid? twenty-eight thousand dollars!

You and I, no doubt, just shrug our shoulders and say, "There's no way I'd buy those things—let alone pay *that much* for them! They aren't worth that much money!"

But here's the startling truth: no matter how much or how little we think such things as pope-hat Doritos or virgin Mary grilled cheese sandwiches should be worth, their value is actually determined by how much someone is willing to pay for them. Since I'm not an economist or the son of an economist, this idea had never sunk into my brain until just recently. I'll state it again: the value of an item is determined by what someone is willing to pay for it. So, for example, if I were to walk into a room containing one hundred people and tell them I have a piece of gum that I'll sell for five hundred dollars and ninety-nine people laugh at me but one person is willing to pay five hundred dollars for the gum, the value of that gum would be five hundred dollars. The value of anything we buy or obtain by trading is determined by what we exchange for it in money or goods.

A corollary to this principle is that when two parties agree to exchange something for something else, this implies that each party deems that the item they are acquiring is of greater value to them than the item they are parting with. Economist Alister Hunt explains it this way:

> When you buy a $5 sandwich, you do so because its worth to you exceeds $5. We know this to be true because no force or coercion is involved. You voluntarily part with something [you consider to be] of lesser value, $5 cash, in exchange for the sandwich that you perceive as having greater value. And the lunch café owner sells it to you because its worth to her is less than $5. Again, we know this is so because nobody is forcing the café owner to sell you $5 sandwiches. You prefer the sandwich and she prefers the $5 cash. Thus, by voluntary trade both parties are better off.[1]

This is simple stuff—Economics 101—but it has tremendous implications as it relates to God, the Cross, and you and me.

The pearl of great price

In the Gospel of Matthew, we encounter a couple of parables Jesus told that are very insightful regarding this topic. To begin with, Jesus tells about a man who is out in a field one day and uncovers a hidden treasure. Thrilled with his discovery, he looks around to make sure no one is watching him and he reburies it. Then the minute he gets home, he empties out his whole house and sells everything he owns. And as soon as he has the money in hand, he goes back to the man who owns the field and buys it from him.

Similarly, Jesus goes on to tell a story about a merchant who goes to a flea market to find pearls. When he comes across a pearl of "great price," he, too, sells everything he owns and returns to buy the pearl. Each man is overwhelmed with his good fortune.

Of course, I can just imagine the wives of these two men. Think about their reaction! "You were walking in a field and now you want to do *what*?" Realizing his wife has a hard time keeping some things secret, the man who found the buried treasure doesn't even tell her what he's found. He just starts selling everything. His neighbors think he's crazy. His in-laws certainly think he's crazy. In fact, everyone thinks he's lost all of his faculties.

But this man knows something, and when the neighbors pick up their newspaper the next day and read that this man has made a fortune, they realize he's the one who gets the last laugh. He parted with things of lesser value to acquire something of far greater value.

So often we read these two parables of Jesus and place ourselves in the position of the two men who sold all to acquire something of greater value. Preachers use them as motivational tools to remind us that we need to be willing to give up everything to follow Jesus. "After all," we are told, "heaven is far more valuable than the things of this world."

This is all well and good, and there is, no doubt, a lot of truth to the idea. As Dietrich Bonhoeffer famously wrote, "When Christ calls a man, he bids him come and die."[2] Jesus *does* invite us to give up all to follow Him. He wants us to be wholly—100 percent—committed to Him and free from anything else that might distract us.

But we miss an important point about these parables when we apply them merely to *our* behavior, to *our* responsibility. The context of the two stories reveals a grander truth. In fact, the two parables seem to be complementing one another. And notice that Jesus begins each of them by saying, "The kingdom of heaven is like . . ." Thus, in these parables, Jesus is giving us insight into the ways of heaven.

Notice that He describes the "kingdom of heaven" differently in each parable. Thus, in the first parable, He declares that the "kingdom of heaven is like a treasure hidden in a field" (Matthew 13:44). Heaven is here represented as a hidden treasure that a man gives up all he owns to acquire. We are correct, then, in saying that this parable is a heartfelt admonition for us to do the same when it comes to our treasures. It's an invitation for us to give up all in order to follow Jesus.

The second parable takes us in a different direction. Jesus doesn't say that the "kingdom of heaven is like a pearl of great price." Instead, He declares that the kingdom of heaven is like a merchant who is searching for pearls. In this parable, then, "heaven" is not what is acquired but the person who does the acquiring. Thus, whereas the first parable shows us a picture of human beings giving up all to acquire heaven, the second parable shows us a picture of heaven giving up all to acquire human beings.

This idea is laced with amazingly good news. To begin with, Jesus doesn't simply invite us to give up all to follow Him and that's that— end of story. If such were the case, we would all have very little hope. Left to ourselves, even if we know where the destination is, we can't get ourselves there. Unfortunately, that describes a great deal of religion: we know the destination; we know what we're supposed to be doing; we know the rules; but we can't do what needs to be done for us to get there. Simply trying harder and then harder still won't do it. Time and time again we've found this to be true.

But amazingly, beautifully, wonderfully, Jesus doesn't ask us to do what He hasn't already done Himself. He doesn't tell us to give up all to acquire heaven without the liberating and motivating good news that He has first given up all to acquire us. When we understand this truth, our hearts burst with gratitude for Him and we find ourselves energized to do that which, before, we found impossible to do. This is why Paul describes the faith experience as that which "works" by love (see Galatians 5:6). The Greek word for "works" is *energeō*—it's the word from which we get the word *energy*—and this shows us that as we embark on our journey of faith, our lives become energized by Jesus' love and we become motivated to do what God asks of us. It's what living by faith is all about.

But these two parables picture an even grander truth. We need to spend a few minutes pondering its implications.

The value of a soul

As we noted at the beginning of this chapter, an item's value is determined by the amount someone is willing to pay for it. This concept may have been a no-brainer for some, but the truth it conveys about our value as human beings is startling. Here's the point in a question: If the merchant in the second parable represents God, what does this say about our value?

Think about it for a second: Jesus said that the merchant "went and sold all that he had" (Matthew 13:46) in order to acquire that pearl. He, in effect, traded all His possessions for something He valued more than them.

Many of us need to allow this concept to sink in. For much of our lives we've felt valueless. We've suffered from low self-esteem. There are countless reasons why people feel this way. Perhaps they were raised in a family whose members didn't show much affection and love. Maybe they were spurned by a person they thought could give them true love and happiness ever after. Or perhaps they didn't get the job promotion they coveted. Popular psychology would have us improve our self-esteem by looking in the mirror and manufacturing good feelings about who we are in and of ourselves. We're supposed to admire our good qualities. So, if we sing well, we should pat ourselves on the back. Or if our IQ is 160, it should be cause for celebration.

There are a couple of problems with this approach. The first is that ultimately, we can't take the credit for any good quality that we have. Every good thing we possess is a gift from God, and to suppose we are responsible for our good qualities inevitably leads to the lethal poison of pride. And not only is this pride misplaced, it is also obnoxious—no one likes to be around proud people.

Second, there will come a time when our voices will fade, our memories will lapse, and our legs will no longer be able to do what they used to do. Our self-worth will nosedive if we've based it on the excellence of our capabilities or attributes. We see the epitome of this reality in the stars of Hollywood and professional sports. It is no wonder that those who have lived a life of glitz and glamour often turn to alcohol, drugs, or suicide when that high-life ends due to their being considered "over the hill" and no longer indispensible.

Jesus invites such people, and all the rest of us as well, to look at the Cross and see there what we're really worth. The only way we can determine our value is by recognizing what the One who created us was willing to pay so we can go on living eternally.

It's really a very simple equation. The apostle Paul tells us that we were "bought at a price" (1 Corinthians 6:20), and the apostle Peter clarifies what that price was: "You were not redeemed with corruptible things, like silver or gold, . . . but with the precious blood of Christ, as of a lamb without blemish and without spot" (1 Peter 1:18, 19). Jesus paid for our lives with His precious blood, which was spilled out in Gethsemane and on the cross. This omni-relational God decided that we were worth that much!

It's mind-boggling when we put it in economic terms. If it necessarily follows that people value the things they're acquiring more than whatever they're trading for those things, what does this tell us about the value Jesus places on us? Make no mistake about it: this tells us that Jesus places a higher value upon us than He places upon Himself! He was more willing to part with His own life in order to obtain eternity for us than to preserve His own life at our eternal expense. Talk about value! If Jesus, being God, is of infinite value, and He willingly gave up His life to purchase our redemption, then we are of infinite value as well.

Of course, many people in effect step back and say, "What a silly purchase to make! Clearly, God doesn't have all His faculties." To many people, what Jesus did seems to be a completely irrational thing to do—as if God betrayed His own logic and died for us despite our worthlessness.

But anyone who is a parent can see the fallacy in this thinking. There's no doubt about it: if my son were being held for ransom by some kidnappers, I would empty my whole bank account to get him back. I would—as my aunt puts it—beg, borrow, and steal to get enough money to purchase his freedom. Yes, I would even offer my life for him. Why? Because he is my son, and I covet his future. I see the value in him and his continued existence. I believe his potential is limitless.

In the same way, God, who is the Parent of every human being the universe has ever known, has the same kind of reason to consider us as having infinite value. We're His children, and He has incredible hopes for our future. How then could Jesus *not* pay for us—even though it cost Him His precious blood? In view of His infinite love, how could He not sacrifice Himself to obtain a glorious future for us with His omni-relational heavenly Father—even at the risk of forfeiting that same future for Himself? And if Jesus has gone through mind-boggling efforts to empty Himself completely in order to provide for our future, don't you suppose that He desperately longs to have us enter into the existence He purchased for us—an existence that entails complete union with Him as the omni-relational One? Talk about a grand and glorious pursuit!

Though in the quotation that follows E. J. Waggoner uses nineteenth-century language, I still like his analogy:

> Why does a man go to the shop and buy an article? He

wants it. If he has paid the price for it, having examined it so he knows what he is buying, does the merchant worry that he will not accept it? If the merchant does not deliver the goods, the buyer will ask, "Why have you not given me what belongs to me?" It is not a matter of indifference to Jesus whether we yield ourselves to Him or not. He longs with an infinite yearning for the souls He has purchased with His own blood.[3]

It is precisely because God has placed such a high value on us and has emptied out all of heaven for our redemption that He is desperate about having us respond to His omni-relational pursuit.

A personal testimony

For the longest time, I struggled to be able to identify with people who suffered from low self-esteem. Whenever people admitted that they didn't feel accepted by God or that they felt they were worthless, I would shrug my shoulders mentally. The problem that plagued me was the opposite one; I struggled with feeling too impressed with myself. But then things changed. Well, actually, very little changed other than me: I finally realized where I was on my own faith journey.

Some friends of mine and I became involved in a discussion that grew into a disagreement and then, eventually, an argument that we continued via e-mail, since we were separated by quite a distance. You know how those things go: you send an e-mail rebutting what someone on the other side says, and some time later you receive a rebuttal from that person, and it goes on and on.

The problem was that what the people on the other side were saying was driving me crazy, and I couldn't do anything but think about how I was going to respond. Things got so bad that I couldn't sleep at night, which very rarely happens to me. I would toss and turn for an hour or so, thinking about counter-arguments to their points and rebuttals to their rebuttals, and on and on it went. This argument was getting the better of me—gnawing away at my spirit, my emotional well-being, and even my health.

One morning, after receiving e-mails from one of these friends with whom I'd been disagreeing the night before, I awoke with tremendous feelings of anxiety. I'd been thinking about the discussion at length the night before, and I didn't get a lot of sleep. So, I went to my prayer journal and started pouring my heart out to the Lord, recognizing that the ongoing argument was affecting me to my very core. I had even tried to quote Bible verses *ad nauseum,* claiming the Lord's promises that He would take care of me and that He would give me strength and courage to face my opponents. Nothing worked. The anxiety simply wouldn't dissipate. I couldn't figure out why I couldn't simply let the disagreement go; why I couldn't simply let my friends have the last say without trying to correct them—why something that was really minor was driving me nuts.

Then the realization of what was happening dawned on me. The core matter of the situation was that I was yearning for my friends to tell me, "Good job! You're right." I wanted everyone to sing my praises. And even more significantly, I was really craving the approval of God. I wanted to know that He valued me. That was something I'd never realized before.

Something I wrote in my prayer journal may give you insight into where I've been.

> Why do I spend so much time worrying about what they think of me? Why do I spend so much time trying to prepare these elaborate explanations as to why they should approve of my thinking or actions? This is a disease, Lord. It's a terrible disease! It's called trying to find my value and worth in anything other than Your death and sacrifice for me. . . . I don't necessarily feel like I need to be heralded or praised profusely. I just need to feel like others are pleased with me. . . . So, I guess the truth is, it's not even a matter of trusting that You can take care of me, or that You can justify me to other people.

It's a matter of understanding and rejoicing in the fact that You are pleased with me, that You accept me, that You approve of me—that my true worth and value come not in the approval of others, not in great accomplishments that I can achieve, but in the fact that You love and accept me and You are "well pleased" with me.

Wow. I never thought I could ever be one of those individuals who doubts that You love and accept me and that You are pleased with me. I never saw that coming.

Then, by God's grace, I was directed to a powerful statement. I have no idea how I came across it, but it was exactly what I needed to read at that precise moment. Meditate upon these words:

> Christ, the physician of the soul, understands its defects and its maladies, and knows how to heal with the purchase of His own blood. What the soul lacks, He can best supply. . . .
>
> Through the goodness and mercy of Christ the sinner is to be restored to the divine favor. God in Christ is daily beseeching men to be reconciled to God. With outstretched arms He is ready to receive and welcome not only the sinner but the prodigal. His dying love, manifested on Calvary, is the sinner's assurance of acceptance, peace, and love. Teach these things in the simplest form, that the sin-darkened soul may see the light shining from the cross of Calvary.[4]

As I read those words, "With outstretched arms He is ready to receive and welcome not only the sinner but the prodigal. His dying love, manifested on Calvary, is the sinner's assurance of acceptance, peace, and love," for the first time in my relationship with Jesus, tears just burst from my eyes. I realized that I was looking to others for affirmation based upon my own merits. I was looking for the acceptance and approval of others based on who I was apart from Jesus. I had been looking for acceptance and love from everyone else but Jesus. I was trying to bolster my own self-esteem by climbing high in the estimation of others. But Jesus was the One to whom I needed to look. He was inviting me to look to Calvary, where I could find my true worth in Him.

What a relief that was to my heavy heart! It was as if my burdens were lifted, my health restored, and I was free to be the person God created me to be. It was an amazing experience! God, in His mercy, was able to help me understand that I am incredibly valuable to Him. I have tremendous worth in His estimation. And all this has been proven by the death of His infinitely valuable Son, Jesus.

CHAPTER FIFTEEN

GOT IT?

Every once in a while I come across people who just seem to "get it"—you know what I mean? People in my congregations who really seem to have caught on to what I've tried to teach them about God and what I understand the Bible to be saying. They do my heart good.

Conversely, one of the things that discourages me most is encountering folks who really *don't* "get it," no matter how much they say they do. Week after week, month after month, and year after year they come up to me after a sermon and say, "Thank you so much, Pastor! That sermon was spot on. It was just what I needed to hear," but I often get the unmistakable feeling that far too often what I have shared has gone in one ear and out the other.

It seems that many of us are in a rut. We saunter mundanely through life, doing just enough to get by. We wake up, eat breakfast, go to work, come home, watch TV, spend a little time with the family, go to bed, and then wake up the next morning and do it all over again. We find ourselves living from weekend to weekend and vacation to vacation and don't do much more with our lives.

Sure, we go to church on the weekends. We sing a few hymns, pay our offering, endure the sermon, and then go home. We might even

135

ponder the sermon for a few minutes on our drive home, but it leaves us largely unaffected—either because it was simply ineffective itself, or because in our lukewarm state we don't allow it to be effective in our lives.

Unlikely as it may seem, we're in good company. Jesus' disciples had exactly the same experience during His three and a half years of ministry. They didn't really "get it." They would often argue about who was greatest and what should be done with the money people had donated. As late as the night before Jesus' crucifixion, the disciples stubbornly refused to take the posture of a servant and wash one another's feet. Instead, Jesus had to stoop down and show them, for the umpteenth time, what His heart was all about and what He hoped their hearts would be all about as well. He must have found it discouraging.

But there was one person who did "get it" during Jesus' earthly life—and that must have brought great joy to His heart. Perhaps seeing that His grace-filled pursuit could actually make a difference in the heart of a human being even encouraged Him to go to the cross.

Surprisingly, the person who did seem to "get it" was someone everybody else would have overlooked.

Mary, Mary, quite contrary

All four Gospel accounts share an interesting story that took place just a few days before Jesus' death. In fact, John says it happened just six days before Jesus went to Golgotha. Jesus was invited to a feast in the house of Simon the leper (who was a Pharisee) in the village of Bethany, just a short distance from Jerusalem on the eastern slope of the Mount of Olives.

Nobody knows for sure, but it seems rather likely that Jesus had healed Simon of his leprosy, and now Simon had planned the supper to express his gratitude to the Savior. So, in grand fashion, Simon welcomes Jesus and His disciples into his home, where Martha and Lazarus—who were more than likely related to Simon—have prepared a feast for Jesus.

As the night proceeds and people sit around making casual conversation, they are interrupted by an eerie sound and a distinct scent. They all stop what they're doing and scan the room to see where the sound and scent are coming from. Eventually, they see that a woman is bent over Jesus' feet. She's crying inconsolably, and she has broken open a perfume bottle and poured the contents on Jesus' feet, where it mingles with tears that are streaming from her eyes. Those beautiful feet have carried Jesus from place to place as He has delivered good news to those who would listen—good news that He brought to her also.

The whole room goes silent. Martha stops serving. The disciples put their bread down. And Simon blushes, embarrassed by what is happening in his house.

Luke tells us that the woman is a "sinner." John identifies her as Mary, the sister of Martha and Lazarus. Some students of the Bible suggest that she is Mary Magdalene, from whom Jesus cast out seven demons. Though we don't know for sure who she is, it seems likely that she is all three—and more. We do know one thing for sure, though—she is overwhelmed with gratitude.

Mary becomes acutely aware that all eyes are on her, and her face flushes with embarrassment. She didn't want to become the center of attention; she meant her anointing of Jesus to be a private act. She had even rehearsed the scenario a few times, hoping the practice would help her keep her composure. But when she finally found herself at Jesus' feet, she couldn't keep the tears back. They came out like a flood, and so the sound of her sobbing spread throughout the house, along with the scent of the perfume.

A penny saved . . .

I remember hearing a sermon in which the preacher imagined what Mary must have gone through in preparation for that momentous act of anointing Jesus. I don't remember everything the preacher said, but I'm going to share some of what I do remember and add a few of my own imaginings.

Mary must have been saving her denarii for a long time. She probably made many sacrifices as she put those pennies aside. But it was worth it. She wanted to do something beautiful for Jesus. She wanted to go over the top, for love knows no bounds.

Eventually, she's saved enough money to buy something nice for Him. As she thinks about what she could buy for Him, she remembers that it's customary to anoint a person of renown with perfume. So she digs up all the money she's been saving and heads to the perfume shop in downtown Bethany.

The shopkeeper recognizes Mary. She's been there before, purchasing cheap perfumes that would help her attract her next "customer." Very gingerly, Mary approaches him and asks for a bottle of perfume.

Knowing Mary's financial background and what she usually bought when she came in, the shopkeeper pulls out a bottle of fairly inexpensive perfume. "I think you'll find this quite satisfying," he says. "For you, it's only thirty denarii."

Mary takes the bottle and samples it. Then she puts the bottle down on the counter and says, "I'm wondering if you have something better."

"Better, Mary?" the shopkeeper asks. He's a little surprised. Apparently, she's looking to spend a little more than usual. He steps back to the case behind him, pulls out another bottle, and brings it to her. "This one costs two hundred denarii," he informs her, sure that she can't afford it.

Mary sniffs the bottle. Its fragrance is definitely more refined than the first one she'd tried. But she asks, "Do you have anything else, anything better? What's the best perfume you have?"

At this point, the shopkeeper is really intrigued. Mary certainly can't afford the priciest perfume he has. Perhaps she just wants to see what the best stuff smells like. So, after a little pause, he retrieves his most expensive bottle of perfume and brings it to Mary, saying, "This perfume comes from the Far East. It's the finest you'll find anywhere; it's fit for a king or an emperor. But it costs three hundred denarii, and I know you can't afford that."

However, Mary knows that's what she wants. Almost before the shopkeeper has finished his last sentence, she pulls her money out and starts counting it denarius by denarius. And as she counts, the shopkeeper's eyes get bigger and bigger. He can't believe how much money she has.

Mary counts out three hundred denarii—it's all she has—and then she says to the shopkeeper, "Please give that perfume to me."

Still in shock, he slowly hands the bottle to Mary. She grasps it firmly and says, "I want nothing less." Then she turns around, and as she is walking out the door, she announces, "I'm going to anoint a king!"

Who knows whether Mary's experience was anything like this? But one thing is certain: Mary didn't settle for anything but the best. What she purchased cost all of her life savings; she did indeed give up all for Jesus.

Does Jesus not deserve our best as well? Can we not respond the same way Mary did, placing ourselves and all that we consider ours completely in His hands?

Surely the Man who emptied out all of heaven deserves our best. The Man who broke His body, just as Mary broke that alabaster bottle, deserves our all. This omni-relational God who has gone on an all-out pursuit of us is hoping we will respond the way Mary did.

Back to the disciples

But to get back to our story . . . the disciples have done a little detective work and have discovered that Mary isn't using any ordinary, run-of-the-mill ointment. She has brought the best stuff. And rather than dabbing a little on Jesus' feet, she has broken the bottle open and poured *all* its contents on Him. She has used the *whole* bottle!

The disciples are indignant—outraged, in fact, according to Matthew, Mark, and John. Judas, the treasurer for the bunch, voices what all the other disciples are thinking: "Why was this fragrant oil wasted? For it might have been sold for more than three hundred denarii and given to the poor" (Mark 14:4, 5).

What a noble idea! After all, Mary is being completely wasteful. Not only has she gone out and bought the most expensive perfume available—it cost about a year's worth of wages—but she has used it all up at once!

As the disciples dissect what Mary has done, loudly upset about her prodigal behavior, embarrassment floods over her, and her tears of gratitude become sobs of shame. She now expects that Jesus will correct her in front of all these people, and she dreads this—even if He corrects her gently. In the infinite gratitude she felt for Jesus, she hadn't stopped to think about what He would think of her profligacy. She had forgotten that He was always emphasizing frugality, that He was always talking about the poor. Her only thought had been about what Jesus had done for her and how much she wanted to show her gratitude to Him. Now she wants to crawl into a hole, never to be seen again. She certainly can't look Jesus in the face. She can't even look up.

Mary's thoughts run back to that other time when she found herself at Jesus' feet. That day, she'd been thrown there by the scribes and Pharisees after she'd been caught in bed with Simon—the same Simon who is hosting this dinner. She remembers the feelings of shame and guilt that overwhelmed her as she anticipated the condemnation that would come from Jesus' lips. But He hadn't condemned her then. In fact, He'd said He had no condemnation for her whatsoever.

She longs for those same words to come from His lips now, but she knows they won't. After all, Judas and the other disciples have a legitimate point, one that Jesus emphasized over and over again. So, with tears continuing to stream from her eyes, she rises unsteadily to her feet, hoping to disappear into the night never to be seen again.

But suddenly she hears the most amazing words come from Jesus' lips. Graciously, but pointedly, He tells His disciples, "Leave her alone."

Mary stops in her tracks. She isn't sure she's heard Jesus correctly. Could He really have said that? Is He not disappointed in her after all? And then, before she's had time to collect her thoughts, Jesus says, "Why are you bothering her? She has done a beautiful thing to Me."

A beautiful thing? she wonders. *Really? I have done a beautiful thing for Jesus? But I was simply showing Him my gratitude, my appreciation.*

At this point Jesus speaks again, saying that there will always be poor people whom they can help, but He won't always be with them, and He adds that Mary has anointed His body for burying. Then He makes one of the most unbelievable statements Mary has ever heard. He tells the disciples, "Truly I say to you, wherever the gospel is preached in the whole world, what she has done will be told in memory of her" (Mark 14:9, NASB).

By now, Mary is really confused. Did Jesus really say what she thinks she heard Him say? Did He really say that her simple act of gratitude would be proclaimed throughout the whole world? Here she was, merely doing a little to show her thankfulness, and Jesus appreciated it so much that He said the story would be spread throughout the whole world!

Got gratitude?

When a Greek or Hebrew word is used in only a handful of places in the Bible, scholars sit up and take notice. Often in such cases, the passages complement one another. In Mark's and John's narratives of the anointing of Jesus, Mary is said to have anointed Him with "an alabaster flask of very costly oil of spikenard" (Mark 14:3; cf. John 12:3). In the New Testament, *nardos,* the Greek word translated "spikenard," is used in only these two places. But, quite interestingly, *nardos* is also used in the Greek version of the Old Testament—the one from which the New Testament writers usually quoted—and all three usages occur in the same book.

The Old Testament book that uses the Greek word *nardos* is the Song of Solomon. In each instance, Solomon used it poetically in connection with the woman in the Song—whom many interpreters recognize as representing God's people. Ultimately, this woman responds to Solomon's relational invitations much the same way that God's people will respond to Him in the last days.

In what is the most intriguing occurrence of the word in Solomon's little book, he writes from the perspective of the woman: "While the king is at his table, my spikenard [*nardos*] sends forth its fragrance" (Song of Solomon 1:12).

It is no coincidence that Mark describes what happened in Simon's house in these words: "And being in Bethany at the house of Simon the leper, as He sat at the table, a woman came having an alabaster flask of very costly oil of spikenard. Then she broke the flask and poured it on His head" (Mark 14:3). John adds that "the house was filled with the fragrance of the oil" (John 12:3). Thus, both Mark and John refer back to the Song of Solomon. Using the same Greek word, they mention not only the spikenard but also its fragrance and the "table" at which Jesus, "the King," sat.

To me, the parallels are strong—which is why Jesus was so thrilled with Mary's selfless act. In it He saw what His followers were capable of. He saw Song of Solomon fulfilled right before His very eyes in the person of Mary, and it encouraged Him to go to the cross—because He realized that if one person could "get it," then a whole host of others could as well. There was hope.

The truth is that Mary was able to carry out her selfless act of giving up all for Jesus only because she understood the beautiful reality that the heavenly Merchant was giving up all for her. At the very time the disciples were lamenting Mary's "wastefulness," she was able to understand that Jesus was going to empty Himself completely for the salvation of lost humanity.

I can't help but think of the following reflection from a wise writer:

> The Lord would be so bountiful to His human family that it could not be said of Him that He could do more. In the gift of Jesus, God gave all heaven. From a human point of

view, such a sacrifice was a wanton waste. To human reason-
ing the whole plan of salvation is a waste of mercies and resources. . . . But the atonement for a lost world was to be full,
abundant, and complete. Christ's offering was exceedingly
abundant to reach every soul that God had created.[1]

Thus, Jesus hopes that, just as the woman in the Song of Solomon
finally responded to the omni-relational invitations of the king, and
just as Mary responded wholeheartedly to those same invitations
from her Savior, so, too, we will respond to Him. We can go all out
in our response to the God who has gone all out for us. We can be
among those who finally "get it."

CHAPTER SIXTEEN

AT-ONE-MENT

Atonement.

Are you familiar with the word? It's a fancy theological term that makes us think of blood, wrath, and death. It turns our minds to Christ's sacrifice on our behalf on Calvary, where He surrendered Himself and served as our Substitute to give us salvation.

Some insist that Jesus finished the work of atonement on Calvary. Because He willingly surrendered His life unto death, God has forgiven us completely and restored us fully to His favor, and that's all His plan for our salvation encompasses.

I believe that Calvary *is* the best single picture of God's omni-relational heart, and of the gospel, that we have. But it's not the whole of it. There's more that God wants to do for us.

Let's take another look at the word *atonement*. What, exactly, does this word mean?

We can't always find the meaning of a word by looking at its individual parts, but in this case, we can. What the omni-relational God of the universe wants is our atonement—our complete and total "at-one-ment" with Him.

This involves more than His just putting a check mark next to our names that says we've been forgiven and now have the right to go to heaven. That's definitely the beginning point, and a very important one, for the whole process—but that's just it: it's a *beginning* point. What God now seeks for us, the very reason He went to the cross in the first place, is to have our hearts completely reconciled and brought into harmony with Him.

Think about this for a moment: imagine that you have a son whom you love with your whole heart but who has been estranged from you. Now imagine that he was arrested for committing some crime, and he's in jail, waiting for bail to be posted so he can be released. No doubt, despite his alienation, you would do all you could to get enough money together to secure his release. However, I'm sure that you would be eager not only to secure his release but also to bring his heart and life back into harmony with you. And I'm sure you wouldn't be satisfied with a few phone calls of appreciation from him a couple of times a month, especially if your relationship is never really mended and his life is still out of harmony with what you value. You would want these things to change because you don't want there to be any barriers between the two of you; you long to have a positive relationship with your son, and you also long for him to be liberated from any behaviors that ultimately hurt him.

This is just a minor glimpse of what God wants. By choosing to sin, all of us bring ourselves into bondage to that sin, and because we have sinned, we deserve eternal death. But God, in His infinite mercy, gave Himself to pay the penalty for our sins. He died the death that we deserve, that we might gain the future that He deserves. All this is very good. But there is a second step that Christ is seeking to take right now. Having secured the right for us to enjoy eternal life, He is now seeking to bring about our complete reconciliation with Him. He isn't satisfied with merely bailing us out of jail. Omni-relational God that He is, He is now pursuing complete at-one-ment with us. He wants our hearts to be so closely connected with His that they beat to the same rhythm.

How does God accomplish this, and what does it look like?

Yom Kippur

The Old Testament describes—and prescribes—the peculiar thing called the "Day of Atonement." The Hebrew phrase is *yom kippur,* and Leviticus 16 is the primary source of information about it.

Roy Gane calls Leviticus 16 "a giant leap for humanity toward the heart of God."[1] That's an interesting way to describe this chapter, especially in light of God's desire to have our hearts beat in rhythm with His, because at first glance Leviticus 16 seems like a chapter that's unlikely to reveal God's heart. After all, it describes—among other things—goats, rams, and bulls being slaughtered, the high priest performing strange ritual cleansings, and the children of Israel "afflicting" their souls. What do these things have to do with God's heart? Or perhaps even more important, the relevant question is: If *this* is what God's heart is all about, why would I want mine to beat along with His?

The truth is that we must read the description of Yom Kippur through the eyes of a Jewish person living several thousand years ago. We must recognize that one of God's supreme principles is that He *always* meets people—including you and me—where they are. He speaks their language so they can understand what He's saying. This is precisely what He was doing through Yom Kippur. He didn't want to have bulls slaughtered or goats set off into the wilderness to die there, but this is the language the children of Israel understood, so it's the language God used to speak to them.

What was He saying through all of it?

Simply put: "I want to be completely 'at one' with you."

God's people had been instructed that whenever they sinned, they were to bring an animal—a young goat or lamb or whatever they could afford—to the sanctuary and sacrifice it. The animal would bear their guilt, and they would be forgiven of their sin. The priest would then take the blood of the animal and bring it inside the Holy Place of the sanctuary, thus transferring the guilt of that sin to the sanctuary itself.

Of course, it should go without saying that this ritual had no power in itself. The sacrificed animal wasn't really an adequate substitute for the sinner. The sacrifice was merely an object lesson, teaching the grand truth that Christ was going to come as the Lamb of God, and He would bear the guilt of the whole world. He was the "Lamb slain" from the foundation of the universe; He is really the One who has taken the sinner's place.

But note this: While sinners were forgiven when they offered their sacrifices, their sins weren't necessarily buried forever. At that point, they were simply transferred to the sanctuary, where they awaited Yom Kippur, when they would be removed forever.

Many people find this puzzling. After all, if God has forgiven us, what more could there be to accomplish?

As it turns out, a lot more!

Forgive and forget

Have you ever noticed how your relationship with someone grows cold when you wrong that person? Even if you ask for forgiveness and the person you hurt forgives you, there seems to be a strain that hampers all of your subsequent interactions with that person. It's almost as if a wall has been built between you and the other person. It's awkward—like trying to ignore a five-hundred-pound gorilla that's in the room with the two of you. Whenever you see this person in church or at the grocery store, you avoid eye contact. You may even try to stay away from him or her. Wronging that person has changed the dynamics of your relationship. Sin tends to create separation and alienation even when wrongs are righted or forgiven. Often, there's no true union of hearts.

This is precisely the problem God faces. Sin has created a barrier between Him and us even though He has forgiven us and continues to forgive us. God wants complete "at-one-ment" with us, but too many times we're content with mere forgiveness. We want to have our legal standing with God changed; we want to have that check mark next to our name that entitles us to heaven; but we don't really want to get on the same page with Him.

That's what Yom Kippur was all about. The Hebrew word *kippur* literally means "to appease," "to cleanse," "to purge," or "to wipe away." This corresponds perfectly with the way we often translate the phrase into English: to "atone," because at-one-ment can be achieved only when the wall that stands between the two parties is "purged," "wiped away"—in other words, removed. This is precisely what God is trying to do.

S. A. Geller puts it this way: "When two people begin to quarrel, each soon resurrects the full inventory of 'sins' the other has committed in the past. For the covenant to remain effective, God must wipe out completely this residual effect of sin . . . and so renew the pristine nature of the bond."[2] God does this not only by removing our guilt from us, but also by removing the very cause of the guilt. Simply put, He wants to "cleanse" us so that we "might be clean from all [our] sins before the LORD" (Leviticus 16:30).

So, two works of cleansing took place on Yom Kippur. While the priest was cleansing the sanctuary from all the guilt that had built up there during the year, the people were also being completely cleansed. The cleansing of the sanctuary was God's way of indicating that He would "remember their sin no more" (Jeremiah 31:34, NRSV), while the cleansing of the people meant all sin in their lives would be removed, thus allowing them to stand with an innocent conscience before God. Both of the procedures that took place on Yom Kippur were geared toward obliterating the wall of separation between God and His people once and for all. This is what God is up to today.

You may be puzzled about what exactly this looks like. After all, how can sinful and selfish human beings truly get on the same page as God—be completely "at one" with Him?

It doesn't take much. All God is asking us to do is to allow Him to teach us how to say Yes to Him whenever He bids us to do something. He isn't asking us to make ourselves holy or sinless. He isn't demanding that we perfect ourselves by our own efforts. He simply invites us to look to His cross, appreciate His love, allow our hearts to melt, and learn how to take Him at His word. The more we allow our hearts to be moved by Calvary's love, the more fully they will be brought into harmony with God's heart, and our complete at-one-ment with Him will be inevitable.

Interestingly, verse after verse in the Bible promises the fulfillment of this desire God has. Paul encourages us to be "confident . . . that He who has begun a good work in you will complete it until the day of Jesus Christ" (Philippians 1:6). Jude beautifully declares that Christ is "able to keep [us] from stumbling" and that He can "present [us] faultless before the presence of His glory with exceeding joy" (Jude 1:24). Elsewhere, John writes of a people in the last days who "follow the Lamb wherever He goes," and who are "without fault before the throne of God" (Revelation 14:4, 5). This is what God's omni-relational heart is moving Him to accomplish on Yom Kippur.

And this is why He pursues us. He wants to have a whole group of people with whom He can achieve complete at-one-ment. He longs for this. We might even go so far as to say that His omni-relational heart is starving for it—to have a people who are so in tune with Him that His aspirations are their aspirations, His desires are their desires, and His actions are their actions.

Of course, most of us may find this idea pretty overwhelming, especially in light of the fact that we have a hard enough time keeping up with the simple necessities of life, and even when we do, we seem to be our own—and God's—worst enemy. But we need not fear. We need not be discouraged by our own faults, our own failings, our own filthy motives. If we truly respond to Christ and His love, our hearts will learn to beat to the rhythms of grace. As Roy Gane puts it, "When I think about *becoming perfect in character*, I start contemplating my faults and become afraid. . . . But when I think of being *loyal to Christ*, the picture changes because my gaze is on Him. He is my example, shepherd, and guardian. I gain courage because all I need to do is follow Him where He wants to take me, including [to] perfection of character."[3]

What will you do?

We've spent many pages pondering the heart of God. We've seen that He pursues us with an everlasting love and that He longs for true intimacy and at-one-ment with us. I have to admit that my heart has been stirred as I have pondered these ideas while putting them to paper. One cannot encounter the omni-relational heart of God without being changed.

So my prayer for you is that you will respond completely to God's pursuing heart. I guarantee you that if you do, your life will be more fulfilling and satisfying than it ever has been. Certainly, you'll still encounter rough patches. Life's problems won't suddenly disappear. But you will have a noticeable peace and joy as you face life's uncertainties. You will be living for something and Someone beyond yourself, which is the only thing that really can lift the human spirit above the fray.

In light of the mind-boggling lengths to which God has gone—and continues to go—in pursuit of you, then, why not open your heart to the pursuing Christ? Why not allow Him to take you up in His arms and carry you where He wants you to go—into total at-one-ment with Him?

ENDNOTES

Chapter One, Pursued by Grace

1. Richard Dawkins, *The God Delusion* (Boston: Houghton Mifflin, 2006), 31.

2. Ravi Zacharias, *The Real Face of Atheism* (Grand Rapids, Mich.: Baker Books, 2004), 13.

3. Charles H. Spurgeon, *The Treasury of David* (Grand Rapids, Mich.: Kregel Publications, 2004), 107.

4. Quoted in Ravi Zacharias, *Can Man Live Without God?* (Nashville: Thomas Nelson, 1994), 170.

Chapter Two, More Than This

1. Quoted in Alister E. McGrath, *Intellectuals Don't Need God and Other Modern Myths* (Grand Rapids, Mich.: Zondervan, 1993), 15.

2. Zacharias, *The Real Face of Atheism,* 85.

3. See Gary Chapman, *The Five Love Languages* (Chicago: Northfield Publishing, 2004), 30.

4. C. S. Lewis, *Mere Christianity* (New York: HarperCollins, 2001), 136, 137.

5. Ari L. Goldman, *The Search for God at Harvard* (New York: Ballantine Books, 1991), 50.

6. Ibid.

Chapter Three, The Divine Motive

1. Quoted in Doris Kearns Goodwin, *Team of Rivals* (New York: Simon & Schuster, 2005), 85.

2. Ibid., 75.

3. Jennifer Jill Schwirzer, *A Most Precious Message* (Nampa, Idaho: Pacific Press®, 2001), 48.

4. Carsten Johnsen, *The Part of the Story You Were Never Told About Agape and Eros* (Yucaipa, Calif.: US Business Specialties, 1982), 53.

5. Quoted in Eric Metaxas, *Amazing Grace: William Wilberforce and the Heroic Campaign to End Slavery* (New York: HarperOne, 2007), 88.

6. Johnsen, *The Part of the Story You Were Never Told About Agape and Eros,* 93, 94.

7. G. K. Chesterton, *Orthodoxy* (Charleston, S.C.: Bibliobazaar, 2007), 70.

8. This story of mine first appeared in print in "Cancer for Two, Love for One," *Adventist Review,* February 17, 2011, 26.

Chapter Four, Free Agents

1. Francis Darwin, ed., *The Life and Letters of Charles Darwin* (London: John Murray, 1887), 1:311, 312.

2. Charles Darwin, *More Letters of Charles Darwin,* eds. Francis Darwin and A. C. Seward (London: John Murray, 1903), 1:94.

3. Quoted in Chad Meister, "God, Evil and Morality," in *God Is Great, God Is Good,* eds. William Lane Craig and Chad Meister (Downers Grove, Ill.: InterVarsity, 2009), 107.

4. Emil Brunner, *Dogmatics II: The Christian Doctrine of Creation and Redemption* (Cambridge, England: James Clarke, 2002), 55.

Chapter Five, Grace Rejected

1. Quoted in Ian Hunter, *Malcolm Muggeridge: A Life* (Vancou-

ver, BC: Regent College Publishing, 2003), 40, 41.

2. Chesterton, *Orthodoxy*, 17.

3. John Donne, "XVII. Meditation," in *Devotions Upon Emergent Occasions* (New York: Cosimo, 2010), 108.

4. Quoted in Ravi Zacharias, *Can Man Live Without God?* 145.

Chapter Seven, Retrocausality

1. Paul Davies, *Cosmic Jackpot* (Boston: Houghton Mifflin, 2007), xii.

2. Ellen G. White, *The Desire of Ages* (Mountain View, Calif.: Pacific Press®, 1940), 660.

Chapter Eight, Lost

1. After assuming I had coined a new term, "omni-relational," I Googled it and discovered that Thomas Jay Oord seems to have introduced it before me. See, for example, his *Science of Love: The Wisdom of Well-Being* (West Conshohocken, Pa.: Templeton Press, 2004), 65.

2. Skip MacCarty, *In Granite or Ingrained?* (Berrien Springs, Mich.: Andrews University Press, 2007), 4.

Chapter Nine, A Day for Us

1. Quoted in Matt Richtel, "Digital Devices Deprive Brain of Needed Downtime," *New York Times,* August 25, 2010, B1.

2. Ibid.

3. Richard Louv, *Last Child in the Woods: Saving Our Children From Nature-Deficit Disorder* (Chapel Hill, N.C.: Algonquin Books of Chapel Hill, 2005), 10.

4. Matt Richtel, "Attached to Technology and Paying a Price," *New York Times,* June 7, 2010, A1.

5. Abraham Heschel, *The Sabbath* (New York: Farrar, Straus and Giroux, 1979), 18.

6. Ibid., 29.

7. Ibid., 12.

8. Goldman, *The Search for God at Harvard,* 54, 55.

Chapter Ten, The Bowing and Bending and Beggarly God

1. Eve Conant, "Row Over the Bow," *Newsweek,* November 30, 2009, 15.

2. Johnsen, *The Part of the Story You Were Never Told About Agape and Eros,* 79, 80.

3. Ellen G. White, *Steps to Christ* (Mountain View, Calif.: Pacific Press®, 1956), 12; emphasis added.

4. Gene Weingarten, "Pearls Before Breakfast," *Washington Post,* April 8, 2007, accessed September 9, 2010, http://www.washingtonpost.com/wp-dyn/content/article/2007/04/04/AR2007040401721.html.

Chapter Eleven, The Cup

1. N. T. Wright, *Surprised by Hope* (New York: HarperOne, 2008), 28.

2. White, *The Desire of Ages,* 225.

Chapter Twelve, God Is Dead

1. William Backus, *What Your Counselor Never Told You* (Bloomington, Minn.: Bethany House, 2000), 56.

2. See Walter C. Kaiser Jr., *The Uses of the Old Testament in the New* (Eugene, Ore.: Wipf and Stock, 2001), 29.

Chapter Thirteen, The Endless Pursuit

1. See http://www.youtube.com/watch?v=mzZ7VkDGuPc.

Chapter Fourteen, Value

1. Alister Hunt, "Wealth Creation and the Kingdom of Heaven," *New England Pastor,* July/August 2009, 4.

2. Dietrich Bonhoeffer, *The Cost of Discipleship* (New York: Simon & Shuster, 1959), 89.

3. E. J. Waggoner, *The Glad Tidings* (Paris, Ohio: Glad Tidings Publishers, 1994), 12.

4. Ellen G. White, *Selected Messages* (Washington, D.C.: Review and Herald®, 1958), 1:178.

Chapter Fifteen, Got It?

1. White, *The Desire of Ages,* 565, 566.

Chapter Sixteen, At-One-Ment

1. Roy Gane, *Leviticus, Numbers* (Grand Rapids, Mich.: Zondervan, 2004), 270.

2. Quoted in ibid., 284.

3. Roy Gane, *Altar Call* (Berrien Springs, Mich.: Diadem, 1999), 332.

God values the most improbable people

Blessed Are the Unlikelies
by Philip W. Dunham

A refreshing look at familiar characters like Samson, Rahab, Nebuchadnezzar, and Gideon that challenges us to look beyond their shortcomings to a place where we can see how the name of God was magnified in their lives. Author Philip Dunham reveals the miraculous transformation that takes place in the heart of each one, and he reminds us that we serve a God who is not willing that any should perish—a God of mercy, love, forgiveness, and grace.
Paperback, 160 Pages
ISBN 13: 978-0-8163-2427-9
ISBN 10: 0-8163-2427-1

20 Questions
God Wants to Ask You
Troy Fitzgerald

The questions God asks of us help us know what's on His mind and heart. They provide opportunities for us to learn to discover what God would have us be and do. Sometimes we think that God exists merely to answer *our* questions—and we become very upset when the answers are not forthcoming. In this book, it will be God asking the questions and waiting for answers. Anyone who has read the Bible knows God's questions transform lives and have eternal consequences.
Paperback, 192 Pages
ISBN 13: 978-0-8163-2275-6
ISBN 10: 0-8163-2275-9

Life-changing encounters with the divine

TROY FITZGERALD

Pacific Press®
Publishing Association
"Where the Word Is Life"